EYEWITNESS
JUDAISM

Amulet

Star of David

Shofar

Kippa

Mezuzah

Yad

Tefillin

Seder plate

Dreidel

EYEWITNESS
JUDAISM

Written by
DOUGLAS CHARING

**Dressed
*Torah***

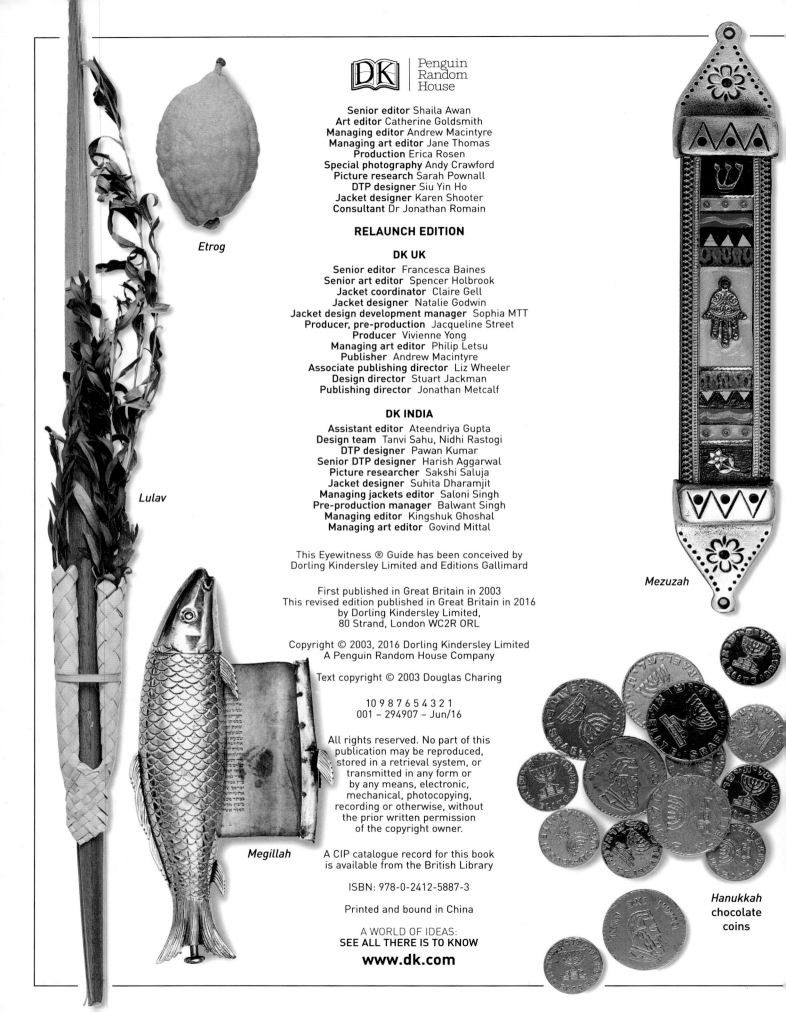

Etrog

Lulav

Mezuzah

Megillah

Hanukkah chocolate coins

DK | Penguin Random House

Senior editor Shaila Awan
Art editor Catherine Goldsmith
Managing editor Andrew Macintyre
Managing art editor Jane Thomas
Production Erica Rosen
Special photography Andy Crawford
Picture research Sarah Pownall
DTP designer Siu Yin Ho
Jacket designer Karen Shooter
Consultant Dr Jonathan Romain

RELAUNCH EDITION

DK UK

Senior editor Francesca Baines
Senior art editor Spencer Holbrook
Jacket coordinator Claire Gell
Jacket designer Natalie Godwin
Jacket design development manager Sophia MTT
Producer, pre-production Jacqueline Street
Producer Vivienne Yong
Managing art editor Philip Letsu
Publisher Andrew Macintyre
Associate publishing director Liz Wheeler
Design director Stuart Jackman
Publishing director Jonathan Metcalf

DK INDIA

Assistant editor Ateendriya Gupta
Design team Tanvi Sahu, Nidhi Rastogi
DTP designer Pawan Kumar
Senior DTP designer Harish Aggarwal
Picture researcher Sakshi Saluja
Jacket designer Suhita Dharamjit
Managing jackets editor Saloni Singh
Pre-production manager Balwant Singh
Managing editor Kingshuk Ghoshal
Managing art editor Govind Mittal

This Eyewitness ® Guide has been conceived by
Dorling Kindersley Limited and Editions Gallimard

First published in Great Britain in 2003
This revised edition published in Great Britain in 2016
by Dorling Kindersley Limited,
80 Strand, London WC2R 0RL

A WORLD OF IDEAS:
SEE ALL THERE IS TO KNOW

www.dk.com

Contents

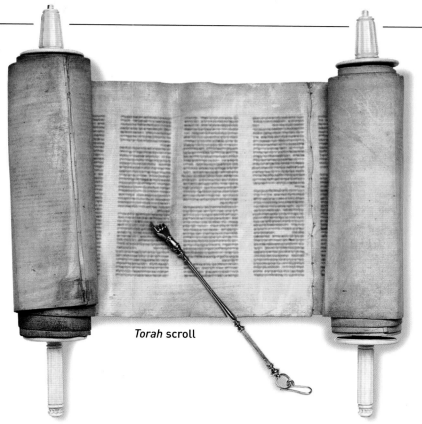

Torah scroll

Being Jewish

Being Jewish can mean many different things. It can simply describe anyone born to a Jewish woman. For many people, being Jewish means following a religious way of life – embracing their faith all day and every day. Yet there are Jews who do not observe Jewish laws, and rarely, if at all, attend synagogue services. For them, being part of the Jewish people or culture is more important.

Karl Marx
Karl Marx (1818–83) was the founder of communism. Although born Jewish, Marx felt nothing for Judaism. Yet he may have been driven by Hebrew teachings in his work as a social philosopher.

A religious group
To be a Jew is to follow the *Torah* (Jewish scriptures). Ultra-Orthodox Jews follow the traditional way of life, while Reform Jews adapt their faith to modern times. Perhaps in their own way, each group can claim to follow the example of Abraham.

"I am a Jew because in every place where suffering weeps the Jew weeps. I am a Jew because at every time when despair cries out, the Jew hopes."

EDMOND FLEG (1874–1963)
SWISS FRENCH WRITER

Baruch Spinoza
Baruch Spinoza (1632–77) was excommunicated because of his non-traditional views. Today, he is seen as one of the greatest Jewish philosophers.

Ultra-Orthodox Jews pray at the Western Wall, Jerusalem

A mutual identity

All Jewish-born people were labelled Jewish by the Nazis – even those who were non-believers (atheists) or who had converted to other faiths. Orthodox Jews and atheists had different views but, tragically, as Jews, they all shared the same fate.

Holocaust memorial for the victims of the Dachau concentration camp, Germany

The day of rest, called Shabbat, is depicted in this stained-glass window

This Hebrew text refers to God creating heaven and earth and resting on the seventh day

Lighting the candles marks the start of Shabbat

Challah bread (plaited loaf) is eaten on Shabbat

Jewish customs

Many Jews observe the social customs and celebrate Jewish festivals even if they do not religiously follow the Hebrew Bible. For some Jews, being part of this rich cultural tradition contributes to their Jewish identity.

A sense of pride

Some religious Jews feel complete with a prayer shawl (*tallit*) over their body and a prayer book (*siddur*) in their hand. But others also identify with fellow Jews throughout the world. Jews feel proud of the State of Israel – their common home. Some Jews feel it is best to go and live there. Others are rooted in the country in which they live, but support the land and people of Israel.

Prayer shawl

Prayer book

How it began

Judaism is one of the oldest world religions, dating back nearly 4,000 years. Jews can trace their origins and faith to a group of people called Hebrews, later known as the Israelites. Abraham is seen as the first Jew, and together with his son Isaac and grandson Jacob, they are known as the patriarchs, or fathers, of Judaism. Their story is told in the Hebrew Bible (Old Testament to Christians).

Abraham is chosen

Although Abraham was born into a society that believed in many gods, he rejected this form of worship and began to worship one supreme God. As a young man, Abraham believed that this God was asking him to leave his home in Harran (in modern-day Iraq) to become the father of a great nation.

Clay goblet

Drinking flask

Sumerian pottery

Archaeological objects such as these help us understand how people lived in biblical times. The stories of the patriarchs are said to have happened between 2600–1800 BCE, with the story of Abraham being the earliest and Joseph's life in Egypt set around 1800 BCE.

A nomadic people

The patriarchs lived a nomadic lifestyle on the edge of the Judean desert. They wandered from area to area in search of water and pasture for their animals.

The Covenant

The Hebrew Bible tells how God made a covenant (agreement) with Abraham, promising him children who would live in a special land known as Canaan. In return, Abraham and his descendants would have to show God their faith and obedience. This ancient clay column (right) bears the names of Abraham and his descendants.

Isaac

As God had promised, Abraham's wife Sarah gave birth to a son, called Isaac. To test Abraham's obedience, God asked him to sacrifice his son. Just as Abraham was about to strike, God told him to kill a ram instead. This story is known as the *Akeda* (Hebrew for "binding"), because Isaac was only bound and not sacrificed.

Abraham and the sacrifice of Isaac

Statue of a high-ranking Egyptian official

The story of Jacob

Isaac had two sons called Jacob and Esau. Jacob was the third and final patriarch. One night, God came to Jacob in a dream and told him that the land he lay on would belong to his descendants. God renamed Jacob "Israel". Later, Jacob had 12 sons, including Joseph, who were to lead the 12 tribes of Israel.

Detail showing Jacob and his 12 sons

Joseph

Jacob's favourite son was Joseph. One day, his jealous brothers sold him to some merchants. Joseph was taken to Egypt, where he worked as a slave. Over time, Joseph rose to a position of importance in the Egyptian court, and would have dressed like an Egyptian official.

Bow *Lyre*

Tunics made of wool

Donkeys were used in biblical times for carrying goods and people

Into Egypt

Joseph was reunited with his family when they went to Egypt to avoid famine in their own land. This Egyptian wall painting from the 19th century BCE shows Semitic-looking people travelling to Egypt, just as Joseph's family had done.

The Promised Land

Nearly 300 years after Joseph's death, the Egyptians turned against the Israelites. So God chose a man called Moses to lead the Israelites out of Egypt and into the Promised Land of Canaan – a journey known as the Exodus. After 40 years in the wilderness, the Israelites reached Canaan, which was later renamed Israel. God promised the Israelites peace and prosperity. In return, they promised to keep God's laws and to show justice and mercy to the inhabitants of Canaan.

Ramesses II
The Egyptian pharaoh (king) at the time of Moses is thought to have been Ramesses II (c.1279–1213 BCE).

Life in Egypt
The Israelites were treated harshly by their Egyptian masters. Along with people from other lands, they were used by the pharaohs as slaves, helping to build their cities and temples.

Egyptian wall painting showing slaves making bricks

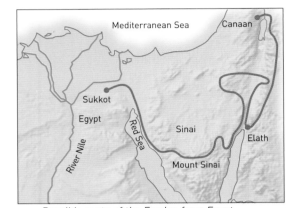

Possible route of the Exodus from Egypt

The ten plagues
When the Egyptian pharaoh refused Moses' plea to set the Israelites free, God sent a series of terrible plagues. During the tenth plague, every first-born Egyptian boy died, including the pharaoh's son. At this point, the pharaoh relented and allowed Moses to lead the Israelites out of Egypt.

Moses leads his people

The sea closes in on the pharaoh's army

Crossing the sea
The pharaoh soon changed his mind and sent his army after the Israelites, who had set up camp by a sea. Terrified, the Israelites turned to Moses, accusing him of leading them to danger. But God parted the sea so they could cross safely, and when the pharaoh's army followed, the waters flowed back, drowning the Egyptians. The people rejoiced, and once again placed their faith in God to lead them to the Promised Land.

> *"I am the Lord your God, who brought you out of Egypt, out of the land of slavery. You shall have no other gods before me."*

ONE OF THE TEN COMMANDMENTS

God's laws
On Mount Sinai, Moses received the *Torah* (God's laws, including the Ten Commandments). These laws were written on stone tablets and were later housed in a special chest, called the Ark of the Covenant.

14th-century Bible illustration showing Moses on Mount Sinai

The Promised Land
As the Israelites approached Canaan, they discovered that its people could not be defeated easily and so they rebelled. Because of their lack of faith, God condemned them to wander in the wilderness for 40 years. Canaan was later conquered by the next generation of Israelites.

Canaanite gods
The Canaanites worshipped many gods, including Baal (below). Such pagan worship was seen as a threat to the Israelite religion.

Fertility goddess

Bronze figure of Baal

The first kings

By the end of the 11th century BCE, the Israelites had been defeated by a group of people known as the Philistines. This led to a call by the people to be ruled by a king, who would unite all the tribes of Israel. Jewish kings were expected to be kind and fair, but many were known for their injustice. It was the prophets who pleaded for religious reform in the country. However, they were often punished for criticizing the king.

Saul is anointed
The prophet Samuel anointed Saul as the first king of Israel. During his reign (c.1025–1004 BCE), Saul founded an army and waged war against many of his enemies. But Saul often disobeyed God. He finally lost his life in battle with the Philistines.

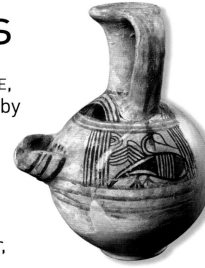

The Sea People
The Philistines, who settled along the coast of Canaan, belonged to a group of people known as the Sea People. The Philistine jug above dates to the 12th century BCE.

Jerusalem, from a 15th-century manuscript

"Praise God, all nations, extol the Eternal One you peoples! For God's love for us is strong, and the truth of God is eternal. Hallelujah!"

PSALM 117

King David's harp may have looked like this musical instrument, called a kinnor

Jerusalem is also known as the City of David

Jerusalem
Jerusalem had been a Canaanite stronghold until a group of people called the Jebusites took over the city. When David captured Jerusalem in 1000 BCE, he made the city the capital of his new kingdom and housed the Ark of the Covenant there.

King David
David, Saul's son-in-law, was the second king of Israel. During his 30-year reign, he joined the tribes together under one rule and defeated the Philistines. David is often shown playing the harp and is said to have been the author of many of the Psalms in the Bible.

King Solomon

Solomon, David's son, was the third king of Israel. The kingdom prospered under his leadership. Solomon was responsible for constructing many magnificent buildings, including the First Temple in Jerusalem. After his death in c.930 BCE, the kingdom was divided between Solomon's son Rehoboam and a military commander named Jeroboam.

This bracelet may have been made from gold stolen by the pharaoh Shishak when he raided the Temple

Judah

The smaller kingdom of Judah in the south was ruled by Rehoboam. During his reign, the Egyptian pharaoh Shishak plundered the Temple in Jerusalem while the Israelites turned to paganism. It was not until the 8th century BCE, that the faith was restored.

Seal belonging to an official in the court of Jeroboam

Israel

Jeroboam ruled the kingdom of Israel in the north. Israel fought with its neighbours, and it was not until the late 9th century BCE that the kingdom became more settled and prosperous. However, this prosperity left Israel open to pagan influences.

Medieval manuscript showing King Solomon reading the *Torah*.

12th-century detail of Isaiah

The prophets

The prophets were a group of people who reminded the Israelites of God's laws. The prophet Isaiah, for example, protested against those who broke religious law and demanded justice for the poor.

13

New rulers

From the mid-8th century BCE, Israel and Judah were conquered by a number of foreign rulers. Each new rule brought changes. Under Assyrian and Babylonian rule, the Israelites were exiled and the Temple was destroyed. Nearly 200 years later, Cyrus the Great allowed the Israelites to return to Jerusalem to rebuild their Temple. But by the end of Greek rule, Judah was plunged into a period of instability.

In the 6th century BCE, the Persian dynasty was a powerful force.

The Assyrians

By 722 BCE, Israel had been conquered by the Assyrian king, Sargon II. In 701 BCE, it was Judah's turn to face the mighty Assyrian army. Lachish, which was southwest of Jerusalem, was destroyed, but Jerusalem was spared.

The reign of Cyrus

In 539 BCE, King Cyrus the Great of Persia conquered Babylon. He allowed the Jews to return to Jerusalem and rebuild their Temple. However, the exiled people did not always get along with the Israelites who had stayed. Despite the tensions in the Jewish community, work on the Second Temple began in 516 BCE.

The entire siege of Lachish was depicted in stone – this detail shows people fleeing

Babylonian empire

In 586 BCE, the Babylonians invaded Jerusalem, destroying the city and Temple. The Israelites were exiled to prevent them from organizing into rebellious groups. The clay tablet above records the fall of Jerusalem.

A reconstructed model of the Second Temple

Persian silver coin used during this period – on one side is an eagle, the other side is a lily

The rebuilding of Jerusalem

In 445 BCE, Nehemiah was appointed governor of Judah, and started rebuilding Jerusalem. He also introduced reforms to strengthen the religion, such as discouraging marriage with non-Jews and banning work on the Sabbath.

Recapture of the Temple

After Alexander's death, Judah was conquered by the Seleucids, who banned the Jewish religion. This led to a revolt in 164 BCE organized by a priest called Mattathias. His son, Judah the Maccabee, recaptured the Temple and restored the Jewish religion. This victory is still celebrated by the festival of *Hanukkah*.

Alexander the Great

In 332 BCE, Alexander the Great, ruler of Macedonia and Greece, conquered Judah, ending Persian rule. He respected the Jewish God, and allowed the Jewish people to run their own affairs. New religious groups emerged at this time, the most notable ones being the Pharisees and the Sadducees. Many Jews accepted Greek culture, but the Pharisees and the Sadducees did not.

This bronze coin comes from the reign of Mattathias Antigonus (40–37 BCE) – the last of the Hasmonean kings

Judah the Maccabee stands triumphant

The Hasmonean dynasty

Judah the Maccabee's victory led to a new line of rulers called the Hasmonean dynasty, which was headed by the Maccabees. Over a period of time, the Hasmoneans started fighting among themselves. Rome, the new emerging power, took advantage of the situation, and ended the Hasmonean dynasty.

Roman rule

Roman bronze helmet, dating from the time when Rome occupied Judaea

The Romans conquered Judah (renamed Judaea) in 63 BCE. During the reign of Herod the Great, the Jews were allowed to practise their faith, but after Herod's rule there were a number of Jewish revolts. Many Jews were deported as a form of punishment. This was the start of what is known in Jewish history as the Diaspora (scattering).

Herod's rule
Although Judaea prospered under Herod, the Jewish way of life was under threat. Herod saw the Hasmonean family as rivals and had several of them put to death. He also placed a golden eagle (a Roman symbol) on the front of the Temple.

Procurators
From 6–66 CE, Rome was ruled by officers, called procurators. Pontius Pilate (ruled 26–36 CE) was the worst of the procurators. He used the Temple's money for building work, and issued coins with a pagan symbol – a curved staff, which was the mark of an official who predicted the future. This was especially offensive to Jewish people.

Pagan symbol

Coin issued by Pontius Pilate

First Jewish Revolt
In 66 CE, during the festival of Passover, Roman soldiers marched into Jerusalem and stripped the Temple of its treasure. The Jews rebelled, taking control of Jerusalem. The Roman general Titus finally crushed the rebellion in 70 CE. His victory was commemorated in a triumphal arch in Rome, Italy.

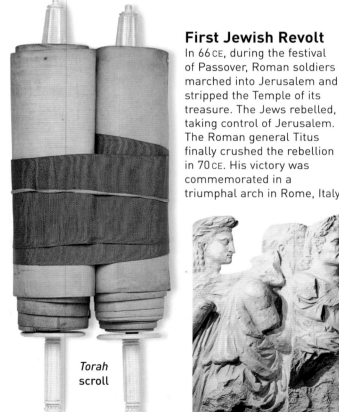

Torah scroll

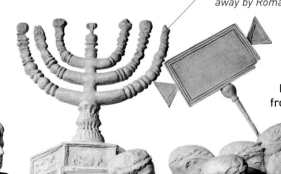

The Menorah from the Second Temple is carried away by Roman soldiers

Detail of the frieze from the Arch of Titus

Rabbinical Judaism
Although Jerusalem was destroyed, the faith was given a new direction. Rabbinical schools developed, and the word "rabbi" (master) was used for the Torah scholars.

Masada

The fall of Jerusalem in 70 CE did not stop the rebels from fighting to the bitter end. The fortress of Masada was recaptured by the Romans after a year-long battle. Nearly 960 Jewish men, women, and children committed mass suicide when faced with defeat.

This arrow still had its handle intact

Arrowhead

The evidence

Excavations at Masada have unearthed objects that belonged to the rebels. Among the findings were these arrows, providing evidence of the fighting that took place.

The mountain-top fortress of Masada is located in the Judaean desert, overlooking the Dead Sea

"Masada shall not fall again."

THE OATH TAKEN TODAY BY ISRAELI SOLDIERS

Emperor Hadrian

Tensions arose once more during the reign of Emperor Hadrian (117–138 CE). Hadrian banned the Jewish practice of circumcision, and embarked on turning Jerusalem into a Roman city.

Relief of Emperor Hadrian

Coin issued by the Bar Kokhba rebels

Second Jewish Revolt

Emperor Hadrian's policies led to the Bar Kokhba Revolt of 132 BCE. The revolt was led by Simeon bar Kokhba, and lasted three years. Thousands of Jewish rebels died, while others were sold into slavery. Jerusalem now had no Jewish inhabitants, as they were not allowed to enter the city.

The Middle Ages

Because Christians blamed Jews for the death of Jesus, Jews often faced great hostility during the Middle Ages. This led to hatred and expulsion from several Christian countries, including England, France, and Spain. Wherever they lived, Jews had to pay special taxes, were forced to wear certain clothing, and were often housed in ghettos - areas that were segregated (set apart).

15th-century woodcut entitled Massacre of the Jews

False accusations
In 1144, Jews in Norwich, England, were accused of murdering a Christian child in order to make unleavened bread for Passover. Jews were also accused of causing the deadly Black Death of 1348 by poisoning wells and rivers. Many Jews were attacked or murdered because they were falsely accused of crimes.

The bell-shaped hat was a mark of disgrace

The mark of disgrace
In some countries, Jews were forced to wear clothes with a badge depicting the stone tablets or the Star of David. Some Jews even had to wear pointed hats. All this was done to single them out from Christians and to humiliate them.

Money-lending
Since the Church forbade Christians to lend money, Jews were forced to become the money-lenders of Europe. Thus a stereotype emerged: the Jew as a greedy money-lender.

Muslim soldiers

Crusaders

The Crusades
By the 11th century, Muslims had conquered many lands, including Spain and Syria. Life for Jews living in these countries improved. But this changed during the Crusades – a series of holy wars waged by Christians against Muslims. In 1099, the Crusaders attacked Jerusalem, killing Jews as well as Muslims.

Christianity versus Judaism

The Christian Church in the Middle Ages believed that the only hope for Jews was to convert to Christianity. The belief in the supremacy of the Church is depicted in the illustration below; the downcast figure of Synagoga represented the Jewish faith, whereas the Church, represented by Ecclesia, was always crowned and standing triumphant.

Interior of the synagogue of Toledo – one of ten synagogues in Spain by the end of the 14th century

The humbled figure of Synagoga

The proud figure of Ecclesia

French manuscript illumination, 13th century

The "Golden Age"

Between the 10th and 12th centuries, Jewish communities in Spain and Portugal flourished under Muslim rule. Jewish culture developed, giving rise to poets and philosophers, who co-existed happily with both Muslims and Christians. But by the end of the 13th century, the Christians regained control of Spain and, although tolerant at first, they forced Jews to convert to Christianity or be expelled.

Martin Luther preaching

Protestant Reformation

Martin Luther (1483–1546), who led the Protestant Reformation, was at first sympathetic to the plight of Jews. But, later, he preached against them, calling for synagogues and Jewish schools to be burned.

Life in the Diaspora

Between the 16th and 18th centuries, Jewish communities were founded in a number of European countries, including the Netherlands, Italy, and Poland. Jews living in these countries enjoyed varying degrees of prosperity and freedom. In Amsterdam, the Jewish community was the richest and largest in western Europe, but in Poland, many Jews lived in poverty and were denied equal rights.

Shabbetai Zevi
Jews believe in the coming of the Messiah, who will pave the way for God's rule. The most famous person to claim to be the Messiah was Shabbetai Zevi (1626–76). When he converted to Islam, many of his followers became disillusioned.

Sephardi Jews
Large numbers of Sephardi Jews (descendants of Portuguese and Spanish Jews) settled in Amsterdam in the 16th century. The Dutch were tolerant towards the Jews, and news of this soon spread. Many of the settlers were highly educated, and soon, both the Jewish community and the Dutch economy flourished.

18th-century Torah mantle used by Amsterdam's Sephardi Jews

The Ark of the Covenant is woven on the mantle

The crown symbolizes the glory of the Torah

Ghettos in Italy
Life for Jews in Italy became increasingly difficult during the 16th century. Many Jews were forced to live in segregated ghettos, which were dirty and overcrowded. Despite this, they were able to follow their faith, and Jewish culture flourished. The picture above shows the Jewish ghetto of Rome, c.1880s.

Ashkenazi Jews outside the synagogue

Ashkenazi Jews in Amsterdam
In the 1620s, large numbers of Jews arrived in Amsterdam from eastern Europe. Many of these Jews, known as Ashkenazi Jews, came from poor backgrounds and lacked the education of the Sephardi Jews. The Dutch artist Rembrandt (1606–69) often portrayed Jewish life in his work, as shown above.

Merchants
During the 17th century, Amsterdam became a major centre for international trade. Jewish merchants became involved in banking, business, and overseas trade. The diamond industry became a Jewish area of expertise – from trading raw diamonds to cutting and polishing the precious stones.

Diamonds

Equal rights for Jews

In 1789, France became the first European country to grant equal rights to Jews. The Netherlands followed shortly afterwards. In other European countries, the demand for freedom and equality continued into the 19th century.

Napoleon is shown granting religious freedom

Oliver Cromwell

Life in Eastern Europe

Many of the persecuted Jews fled to Poland during the 1500s. By the mid-1600s, nearly 500,000 Jews lived in this tolerant country. The majority of Polish Jews lived in impoverished, close-knit communities known as *shtetls*.

The Jews of England

Jews had been expelled from England in 1290. In the mid-1650s, Manasseh Ben-Israel (1604–57), a Sephardi scholar from Amsterdam, petitioned Oliver Cromwell (1599–1658) to readmit Jews. Cromwell realized that Jews could be of value to the economy, and permitted their readmission in 1656. It was not until 1829 that English Jews were granted citizenship.

Scene from the film *Fiddler on the Roof*, based on the life of a *shtetl* community

The pogroms

During the 18th century, Poland was conquered by Russia, Austria, and Prussia. Nearly all Polish Jews came under Russian rule – which meant that over half the world's Jewish population now lived in Russia. The Russian tzars (kings) forced the Jews to live in an impoverished area called the Pale of Settlement. Tzar Alexander II (1818–81), however, was more tolerant towards the Jews and allowed them to live outside the Pale. But his assassination marked a turning point in the history of Russian Jews. It led to attacks, known as the pogroms (Russian word meaning "devastation"), and thousands of Jews fled in panic.

The Russian tzars
Alexander II reigned from 1855 to 1881. His assassination was blamed on Jews, but it is more likely that he was killed by his own people. The new tzar, Alexander III (1845–94), was unsympathetic to the Jews. Anti-Jewish attacks broke out, which were both organized and encouraged by the authorities.

The pogroms
The first wave of pogroms (1881–84) resulted in the deaths of hundreds of Jews. Their homes and synagogues were also looted and vandalized. In 1882, Alexander III passed the May Laws, which imposed restrictions on Jews. The second wave of pogroms (1903–06) followed a similar pattern of death and destruction.

Torah *scrolls vandalized during the pogroms are buried by Jews*

Frightened Jews start to leave Russia

Jewish response
There was very little Jews could do to protect themselves during the pogroms. Some left Russia, while others rallied behind the socialists, who wanted to change the way Russia was ruled. Many of the socialist leaders were Jewish, and this fuelled further attacks on Jews.

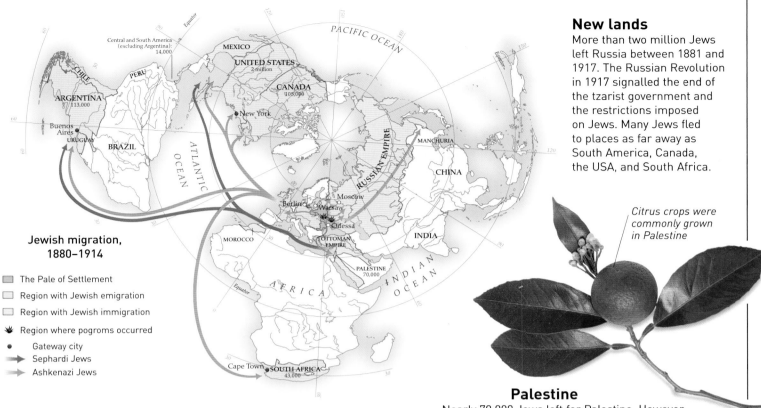

Jewish migration, 1880–1914

- ■ The Pale of Settlement
- ■ Region with Jewish emigration
- ■ Region with Jewish immigration
- ✹ Region where pogroms occurred
- ● Gateway city
- ➔ Sephardi Jews
- ➔ Ashkenazi Jews

New lands

More than two million Jews left Russia between 1881 and 1917. The Russian Revolution in 1917 signalled the end of the tzarist government and the restrictions imposed on Jews. Many Jews fled to places as far away as South America, Canada, the USA, and South Africa.

Citrus crops were commonly grown in Palestine

Palestine

Nearly 70,000 Jews left for Palestine. However, faced with difficult conditions, only half this number remained. The French Jewish benefactor Baron de Rothschild (1845–1934) bought land for the settlement of Jews, and introduced new crops to the region.

Jewish immigrants in the USA

United States of America

In the late 1800s, thousands of Russian Jews arrived at the docks of Manhattan hoping for a better life. The USA accepted more Jews than any other country, and, by 1929, nearly 5 million Jews had moved to the safe haven of America.

The new life

The immigrants settled in cities, such as New York, where they lived in crowded neighbourhoods. New York's East Side was a typical Jewish neighbourhood – nearly 350,000 Jews lived in this small area.

The Jewish market on New York's East Side, c.1900s

Zionism

The biblical word Zion is often used to refer to the Land of Israel. Zionism is the political movement that gained support in the 19th century as a result of the pogroms and anti-Semitic views witnessed during the trial of a French Jew, Alfred Dreyfus. The Zionists believed that the only way to avoid persecution was to have their own homeland – the Land of Israel. During World War I, Great Britain took control of Palestine and made a promise to back Jewish settlement in Palestine.

Call for a homeland

In 1882, Leon Pinkser (1821–91) wrote his pamphlet *Autoemancipation* (above). He described anti-Semitism as a disease and said that Jews should be allowed to create a homeland. The idea of Zionism dates back nearly 2,500 years, when the exiled Jews of Babylon yearned to return to their homeland.

Alfred Dreyfus had his stripes removed and his sword broken as part of a military humiliation

The Dreyfus Affair

Alfred Dreyfus (1859–1935), a Jewish captain in the French army, was wrongly accused of treason in 1894. He was found guilty and imprisoned for life. It was not until 1906 that Dreyfus was finally cleared of all blame.

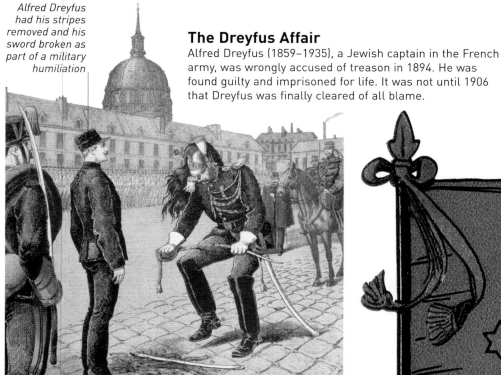

The solution

Theodor Herzl (1860–1904), a Hungarian Jew, was shocked by the anti-Semitic treatment of Alfred Dreyfus. Herzl realized the need for a solution to anti-Semitism, even in countries in which Jews had been granted equal rights. In 1896, he published his book, *The Jewish State*. In it, Herzl called for the establishment of a Jewish state in Palestine, saying this was the only solution.

Theodor Herzl, who helped to found the Zionist movement

Herzl's suggestion for a Jewish flag was adopted by the Zionist Congress

The First Zionist Congress

Herzl was instrumental in setting up the First Zionist Congress in 1897. The Congress called for the resettlement of Jews in Palestine, and set up the World Zionist Organization to put its goals into practice.

גאולה תתנו לארץ
ע"י קרן קימת לישראל

אל תאמר מחר נגאל. שמא מחר את המעיר.
אוסישקין

...ה ושערה וגפן ות...
...ת שמו ודבש...

Poster issued by the Jewish National Fund, calling for a return to the Land of Israel

Resettlement

In 1901, the Jewish National Fund was established to buy land in Palestine. One group of Jewish immigrants set up a farming community, called a *kibbutz*, where all the work and produce was shared equally.

Tel Aviv in the 1920s

City developments

In 1909, the town of Tel Aviv was founded to house Jewish immigrants. It was the first all-Jewish city. The settlers were given funds for the building work, which they carried out themselves. By 1914, the flourishing city had over 1,000 people. In the same year, the number of Jewish inhabitants in Jerusalem rose to 45,000.

The Balfour Declaration

In 1917, the British Foreign Secretary Lord Arthur Balfour drafted the Balfour Declaration, which recognized the right of Jews to live in Palestine. This was a major landmark for the Zionists. In 1918, Britain took control of Palestine, which had been part of the Turkish Ottoman Empire since 1516, and became responsible for carrying out the Declaration.

A commemorative version of the Balfour Declaration

A new nightmare

In 1933, Adolf Hitler (1889–1945) became chancellor of Germany. This was the start of a slowly unfolding tragedy for Jews throughout the world. Hitler's Nazi Party was driven by its programme of hate – the elimination of Jews. Anti-Jewish laws were passed, and many Jews were attacked or murdered. By 1937, over one hundred thousand Jews had fled from Germany.

Nazi poster
This Nazi poster reads, "One Europe's freedom", promoting the idea that Nazi rule was the only answer for Europe.

Economic steps
In April 1933, the Nazis organized a one-day boycott of Jewish shops. Guards stood outside Jewish shops, and signs were placed outside warning people not to enter. The sign above reads, "Germany! Resist! Do not buy from Jews!"

Spreading lies
A campaign of lies (propaganda) played a crucial part in the success of the Nazi regime. Leaflets, radio, films, and posters were used to show Jews as an inferior race and the cause of Germany's economic problems. A minister of propaganda was also appointed to promote the lies.

Detail from a Nazi leaflet designed to imply that Jews had built walls to divide people

Burning books
In 1933 and 1936, the Nazis raided libraries and bookshops. Thousands of books were taken away. Many were written by Jews, but there were also books by non-Jewish writers who disagreed with Nazi policies. The German people were encouraged to show their anti-Semitic feelings by burning the books.

Passport of a Jewish woman

The "J" stamp

By the end of 1933, nearly 38,000 Jews had left Germany, mainly bound for England or the USA. Between 1934 and 1939 a further 210,000 left. Their travel documents were stamped with the letter "J" in an attempt to humiliate them. But these people were the lucky ones. After 1939, Jews were not able to leave Germany.

Anti–Semitism in schools

In schools, books were rewritten to further the cause of anti-Semitism. German children were taught that they belonged to the Aryan race (a "superior", fair-skinned, fair-haired race). By 1939, all children under 18 had to join the Nazi Youth Organization. Eventually, both Jewish teachers and children were forced out of German schools.

This detail from a Nazi school book shows German children as the superior race

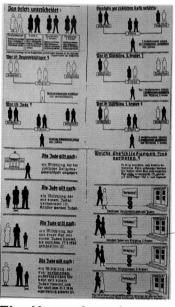

The Nuremberg Laws

The Nazis introduced laws to restrict the freedom of Jews. The worst of these were known as the Nuremberg Laws of 1935. Jews were banned from marrying non-Jews and from taking up professional jobs such as teaching. The aim was to isolate Jews from all aspects of German life.

Kristallnacht

In 1938, the Nazis launched a full-scale attack on Jewish communities. Synagogues were set on fire, and Jewish homes, shops, and factories were vandalized. This destruction was known as *Kristallnacht* (meaning "night of the broken glass"). Thousands of Jews were arrested and many were murdered. Soon, nearby countries were invaded by the Nazi army. Jews in these countries were subjected to the same brutality and persecution faced by German Jews.

Detailed charts were issued to show how to implement the Nuremberg Laws

The charred remains of a synagogue

A burning synagogue in Berlin

The Holocaust

The term "Holocaust" is used to describe the mass murder of Jewish people by the Nazis during World War II (1939–45). Six million Jews were murdered, along with other people considered to be undesirable. Jews living in countries under Nazi rule were rounded up and confined to ghettos until they could be taken to labour or death camps. Despite the hopelessness of the situation, Jewish resistance groups emerged, and many non-Jewish people risked their lives to help.

The yellow star
From 1942 onwards, all Jews in Nazi-occupied Europe had to wear the yellow Star of David. This was designed to degrade all Jews. The yellow colour symbolized shame.

Auschwitz concentration camp

The Warsaw ghetto uprising
In 1943, a group of Jewish fighters in the Warsaw ghetto in Poland attacked German soldiers. In retaliation, the Germans burned down buildings in the ghetto, killing more than 7,000 Jews. Those who survived were sent to the death camps.

Concentration camps
At first, the Nazis set up mobile death units to kill Jews. Later, concentration camps were built for mass killings. The main death camps were in Poland, notably Auschwitz and Treblinka. Up to 12,000 Jews a day were killed at Auschwitz.

Survivors are rounded up by the Nazis

This tin from Auschwitz contained cyanide gas crystals

The gas chamber
The Nazis perfected their extermination method at Auschwitz. In 1941, gas crystals were used to kill some of the victims in a makeshift gas chamber. By the end of 1942, the Nazis had two gas chambers working day and night. Then, in 1943, the Nazis built four gas chambers that could kill 2,000 people at once.

The story of Anne Frank

Anne Frank's family moved from Germany to Amsterdam to escape Hitler's anti-Jewish policies. In 1942, when Anne was 13, the family went into hiding. During this time, Anne kept a diary. Most of the Frank family, including Anne, perished in Auschwitz after the Nazis discovered their hiding place. Anne's diary was found after the war and was published in 1947.

Anne Frank

The diary kept by Anne Frank

Prisoners at Auschwitz

Upon arrival, men, women, and children were made to wear filthy uniforms. Conditions at the camp were so terrible many prisoners died as a result.

"If I just think of how we live here, I usually come to the conclusion that it is a paradise compared with how other Jews who are not in hiding must be living."

ANNE FRANK

The uniform

The prisoners of Auschwitz had numbers tattooed on their left forearms for identification. Names were not used, because the aim was to dehumanize the victims. Prisoners wore uniforms that had a triangular badge sewn on the front.

The remains of Schindler's factory, Poland

Oskar Schindler

Acts of heroism

Thousands of individuals risked their lives to help save the lives of Jews. The Swedish diplomat Raul Wallenberg (1913–45) used his position to issue false documents and passports. A French monk called Pierre-Marie Benoît (1895–1990) helped smuggle thousands of Jewish children out of France. Oskar Schindler (1908–74), a German factory owner, employed Jewish prisoners. By doing so, he saved more than one thousand people from certain death.

The aftermath

The survivors

It is thought that about 200,000 Jewish people survived the Holocaust, either by hiding or pretending to be non-Jews. Some children were looked after by Christian families. Others were taken to convents. The picture above is of Henri Obstfeld, who survived by being hidden from the Nazis.

This story book was sent to Henri by his parents when he was hiding

World War II ended in May 1945. The aftermath revealed that one-third of the world's Jewish population had been killed during the Holocaust. The war also displaced millions of Jewish people throughout Europe. Once again, the call for a Jewish homeland gathered momentum, resulting in the creation of the State of Israel in 1948. Sadly, this did not bring the peace and security that was hoped for.

Displaced Persons

The war left more than 1.5 million people without homes. Known as Displaced Persons, nearly 250,000 of these were Jews. Sadly anti-Semitism did not end with the war. Many Jews returning to Poland were attacked. The majority of survivors found refuge in Displaced Persons' camps, where they were provided with much-needed food and medicine.

Mother with her children at a Displaced Persons' camp

Zionist poster calling for survivors to go to Palestine instead of other countries

New homes

Five years after the Holocaust, there were still survivors with nowhere to go. The Zionists hoped to resettle as many of the Displaced Persons as possible in Palestine. But Britain would only admit 13,000 Jews into Palestine. As a result, nearly 70,000 Holocaust survivors were smuggled into Palestine, often through dangerous routes.

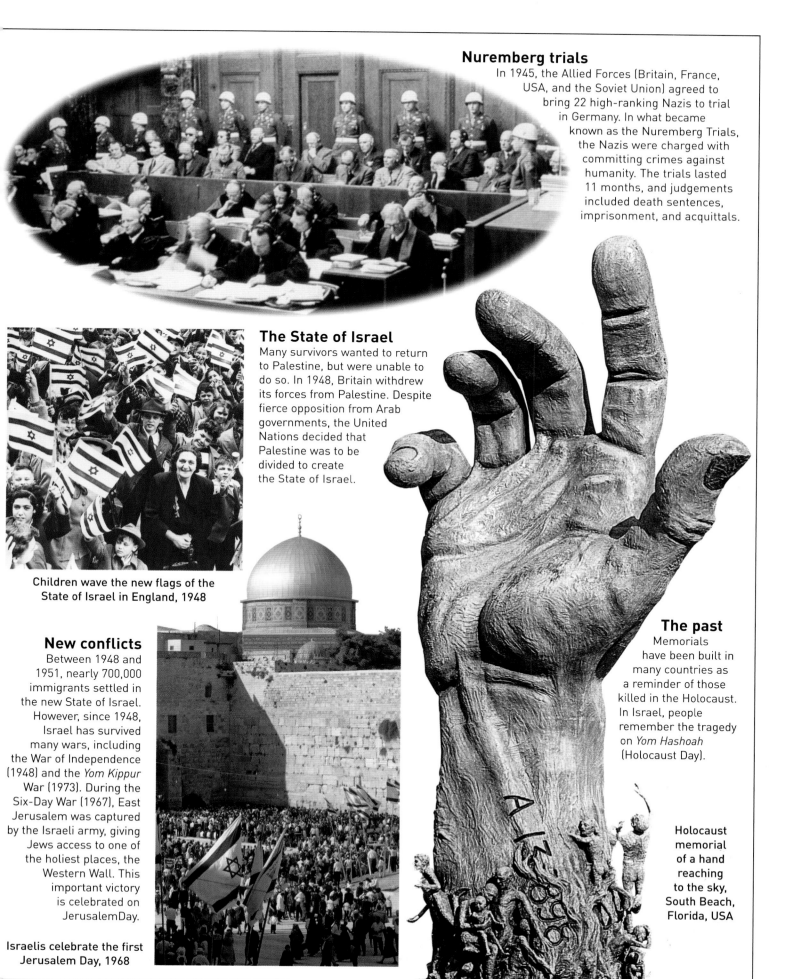

Nuremberg trials

In 1945, the Allied Forces (Britain, France, USA, and the Soviet Union) agreed to bring 22 high-ranking Nazis to trial in Germany. In what became known as the Nuremberg Trials, the Nazis were charged with committing crimes against humanity. The trials lasted 11 months, and judgements included death sentences, imprisonment, and acquittals.

The State of Israel

Many survivors wanted to return to Palestine, but were unable to do so. In 1948, Britain withdrew its forces from Palestine. Despite fierce opposition from Arab governments, the United Nations decided that Palestine was to be divided to create the State of Israel.

Children wave the new flags of the State of Israel in England, 1948

New conflicts

Between 1948 and 1951, nearly 700,000 immigrants settled in the new State of Israel. However, since 1948, Israel has survived many wars, including the War of Independence (1948) and the *Yom Kippur* War (1973). During the Six-Day War (1967), East Jerusalem was captured by the Israeli army, giving Jews access to one of the holiest places, the Western Wall. This important victory is celebrated on JerusalemDay.

Israelis celebrate the first Jerusalem Day, 1968

The past

Memorials have been built in many countries as a reminder of those killed in the Holocaust. In Israel, people remember the tragedy on *Yom Hashoah* (Holocaust Day).

Holocaust memorial of a hand reaching to the sky, South Beach, Florida, USA

The synagogue

The synagogue is an important place of worship and the centre of Jewish life. When Jerusalem's Second Temple was destroyed in 70 CE, the rabbis developed the idea of a house of worship in order to keep the faith alive. The importance of the Temple has never been forgotten. Even today, when a synagogue is built, a section of a wall is sometimes left unplastered to serve as a reminder of the Temple's destruction.

Each minaret stands 43 m (141 ft) tall

A place for study and prayer
The synagogue is also known as *Bet Hamidrash* ("House of Study"). This refers to the close relationship between prayer and *Torah* study. Synagogues hold classes in which older boys and young men can study religious texts.

An ornate synagogue
The Dohany Synagogue in Budapest, Hungary, is the largest in Europe. Built in 1859, the synagogue is influenced by Islamic architecture.

Model of the Kaifeng Synagogue

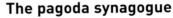

The pagoda synagogue
One of the most unusual houses of worship was the Kaifeng Synagogue built in China in 1163. By the mid-1800s, the Jewish community in China had declined, and the synagogue was demolished.

Hechal Yehuda Synagogue

A modern synagogue
This Sephardi synagogue in Tel Aviv, Israel, was designed for a hot climate. Built from concrete, the white, shell-like exterior reflects the heat, while cool air circulates around the cavernous interior.

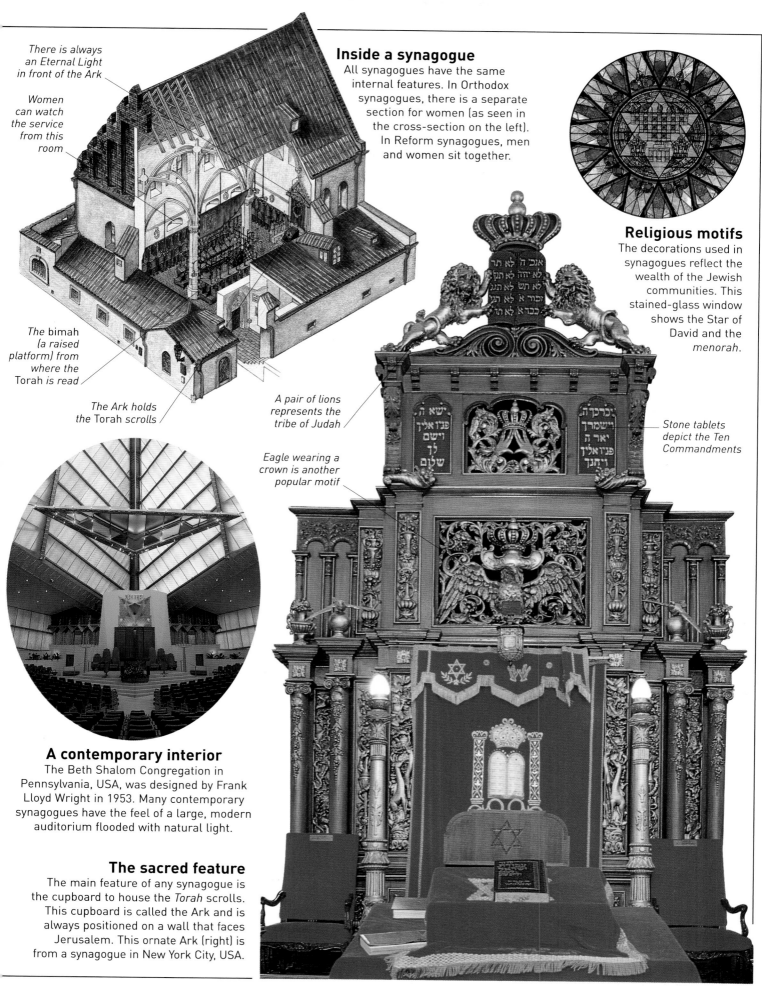

There is always an Eternal Light in front of the Ark

Women can watch the service from this room

The bimah (a raised platform) from where the Torah is read

The Ark holds the Torah scrolls

Inside a synagogue
All synagogues have the same internal features. In Orthodox synagogues, there is a separate section for women (as seen in the cross-section on the left). In Reform synagogues, men and women sit together.

Religious motifs
The decorations used in synagogues reflect the wealth of the Jewish communities. This stained-glass window shows the Star of David and the *menorah*.

A pair of lions represents the tribe of Judah

Eagle wearing a crown is another popular motif

Stone tablets depict the Ten Commandments

A contemporary interior
The Beth Shalom Congregation in Pennsylvania, USA, was designed by Frank Lloyd Wright in 1953. Many contemporary synagogues have the feel of a large, modern auditorium flooded with natural light.

The sacred feature
The main feature of any synagogue is the cupboard to house the *Torah* scrolls. This cupboard is called the Ark and is always positioned on a wall that faces Jerusalem. This ornate Ark (right) is from a synagogue in New York City, USA.

Prayer

There are three daily prayer services in Judaism. Prayers can be recited alone, but it is preferable to pray with a group of at least ten people (or ten men in an Orthodox community), called a *minyan*. The prayers are contained in a book called a *siddur*, and the most famous prayer is the *Shema*, which declares the supremacy of God. Although there is no law dictating dress code, male Jews normally wear a head covering, known as a *kippa*, and a *tallit* (prayer shawl) to pray.

Mezuzah
The *mezuzah* is a small container holding a piece of parchment on which the *Shema* is written. It can be made of any material and is often highly decorated. The *mezuzah* is placed on the front door of a Jewish house.

"Hear, O Israel, the Lord is our God, the Lord is one."

FIRST LINE OF THE SHEMA

Tallit
The *tallit*, worn during prayer, has tassels (*tzitzit*) on each of the four corners. The Book of Exodus mentions the wearing of these tassels as a visible sign of obedience to God.

Kippa
The *kippa* (left) is worn to show respect for God. It reminds the wearer that God is constantly present.

Western Wall
The only remaining part of the Second Temple in Jerusalem is the Western Wall (also known as the Wailing Wall). It is Judaism's holiest site and dates to the 1st century CE. People come to pray at the wall and often leave written messages in the spaces between the stones.

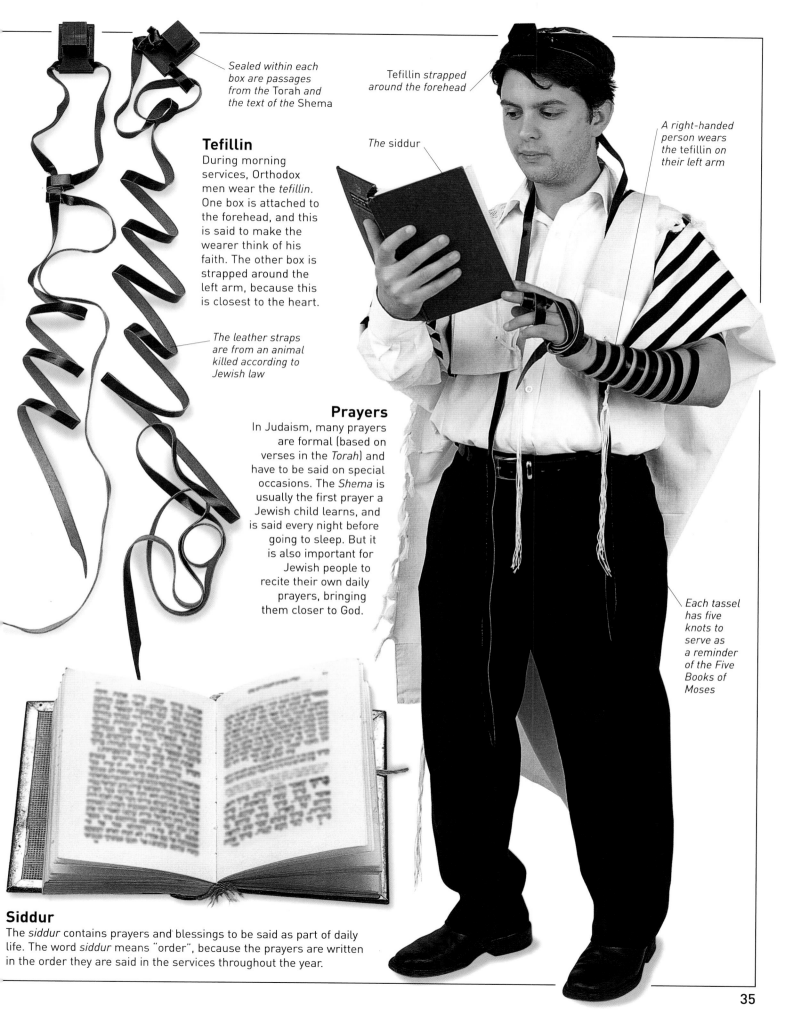

Sealed within each box are passages from the Torah *and the text of the* Shema

Tefillin strapped around the forehead

Tefillin

During morning services, Orthodox men wear the *tefillin*. One box is attached to the forehead, and this is said to make the wearer think of his faith. The other box is strapped around the left arm, because this is closest to the heart.

The siddur

A right-handed person wears the tefillin *on their left arm*

The leather straps are from an animal killed according to Jewish law

Prayers

In Judaism, many prayers are formal (based on verses in the *Torah*) and have to be said on special occasions. The *Shema* is usually the first prayer a Jewish child learns, and is said every night before going to sleep. But it is also important for Jewish people to recite their own daily prayers, bringing them closer to God.

Each tassel has five knots to serve as a reminder of the Five Books of Moses

Siddur

The *siddur* contains prayers and blessings to be said as part of daily life. The word *siddur* means "order", because the prayers are written in the order they are said in the services throughout the year.

Sacred books

The Hebrew Bible consists of three books: the *Torah* (meaning "teaching"), *Nevi'im* (the Prophets), and *Ketuvim* (the Writings). The *Torah*, also known as the Five Books of Moses, is the most important book. Jews believe that the words of the *Torah* are the words of God as revealed to Moses on Mount Sinai. As well as describing the early history of the Jewish religion, the *Torah* gives instructions on all aspects of daily life.

The Five Books
Genesis is the first of the five books of the *Torah*. It tells the stories of Adam and Eve (above) and the patriarchs – Abraham, Isaac, and Jacob. Exodus, Leviticus, Numbers, and Deuteronomy form the rest of the *Torah*.

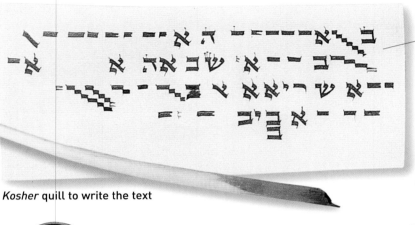

Sample parchment with Hebrew letters and signs

Kosher quill to write the text

Tools of the trade
Special tools and ink are used when writing a *Torah* scroll. The quill and parchment have to come from *kosher* animals that are killed in accordance with Jewish law.

Special ink

The scribe
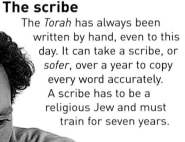

The *Torah* has always been written by hand, even to this day. It can take a scribe, or *sofer*, over a year to copy every word accurately. A scribe has to be a religious Jew and must train for seven years.

The text is written in columns

Dead Sea Scrolls

In 1947, fragments of ancient manuscripts were discovered in the caves of Qumran, near the Dead Sea, Israel. They consisted of text from almost every book of the Hebrew Bible. Written between 150 BCE and 68 CE, the manuscripts would have belonged to the Essene community – an ancient Jewish sect.

This inkpot was found in Qumran and may have been used by the scribes

The yad

The *yad* (right), meaning "hand" in Hebrew, is used by the person reading from the *Torah* to point to the words. This is to preserve the handwritten text and prevent it from being damaged.

The Torah

The *Torah*, the holiest book in Jewish life, contains 613 commandments. These are instructions on how to live a good and religious life. Orthodox Jews adhere strictly to all the laws of the *Torah*. There are also many Jews who follow these laws because they feel they apply to modern life.

The Torah scroll is raised after the service and shown to the congregation

Handles are always used to unroll or hold the scroll

Reading the Torah

The *Torah* scroll is read over the course of a year with a section chanted each week in the synagogue. Everyone stands up when the *Torah* is taken out of the Ark.

37

Writings

The importance of learning has always been valued in Judaism. After the *Torah*, the *Talmud* has become the most important religious book. It was created over the years as thousands of rabbis and scholars studied the *Torah* and recorded their interpretations. Other significant religious books include the *Kabbalah*, the *Midrash*, and the *Haggadah*, which recounts the story of the Exodus from Egypt and is an integral part of Jewish life.

Noah's ark

The Midrash

The *Midrash* is a collection of writings compiled by rabbis. They help explain biblical stories such as Noah's ark, and aim to teach moral lessons.

The Talmud

The *Talmud* is a compilation of Jewish laws with explanations provided by Jewish scholars. Completed in the 5th century, the writings cover every aspect of Jewish life, from prayers to business disputes. Subsequent rabbis added their own commentaries.

Commentaries from various rabbis appear around the page

The main text is always in the centre of the page

"What is hateful to you do not do to your neighbour. That is the whole Torah – the rest is commentary."

TRACTATE SHABBAT 31A,
THE TALMUD

Maimonides

Spanish-born Rabbi Moses ben Maimon (1138–1204), known as Maimonides, was a distinguished philosopher and physician. While living in Egypt, he wrote the *Mishnah Torah*, a review of all Jewish religious laws based on the *Talmud*.

> *"Before God manifested Himself, when all things were still hidden in Him He began by forming an imperceptible point – that was His own thought. With this thought He then began to construct a mysterious and holy form – the Universe."*
>
> *THE* ZOHAR

The Haggadah

The *Haggadah* (meaning "narrative") recounts the story of the Exodus and is always read before the Passover meal. This illustration from a children's *Haggadah* shows the ten plagues sent by God to punish the Egyptians.

This is one of the earliest examples of an Ashkenazi Haggadah

The Book of Splendour

The term *Kabbalah* (meaning "tradition") represents an alternative mystical view of the world based on the *Torah*. The *Zohar*, or *Book of Splendour*, is the most important text for followers of the *Kabbalah*. It is attributed to Moses de Leon, a *Kabbalist* who lived in Spain during the 13th century.

Sefirot

In the *Zohar*, the *Kabbalah* is explained in terms of ten creative forces known as the *sefirot*. These are shown as branches of a tree, and include love, wisdom, power, beauty, and intelligence.

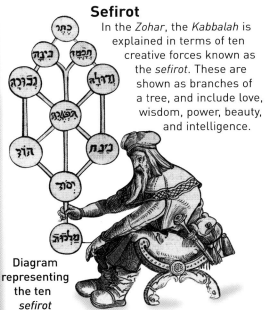

Diagram representing the ten *sefirot*

Bird's head Haggadah

This famous *Haggadah* from 13th-century Germany (left) is illustrated with biblical scenes. Most of the human figures are drawn with birds' heads.

Values

Prophet Jeremiah

Justice and equality
In biblical times, it was the duty of the *Sanhedrin* (the Jewish Supreme Court) to interpret the laws of the *Torah* and apply them fairly. The prophets also rebuked those who were seen to act against the interests of the people.

For many Jews, the *Torah* is more than just learning about the early history of Judaism and following a set of religious beliefs. It also provides a moral guide on how to live a good and honest life. The *Torah* emphasizes values such as justice, equality, kindness, and generosity, and stresses the importance of education and social responsibility. One of the most frequent commands in the *Torah* is the *mitzvah* (commandment) of showing kindness to strangers. Above all, Judaism emphasizes the value of human life and the belief that the life of one person is no less important than the life of another.

Respect for life
The value of human life is central to Judaism. This respect for life also extends to animals. One of the oldest laws forbidding cruelty to animals is found in the *Torah*. In many Jewish homes, the creation of the world is remembered during *Shabbat*.

Hospitality
The obligation to look after travellers and strangers is one of the most important commands in the *Torah*. Abraham and his wife Sarah were always hospitable and set the tone for future generations. During the Middle Ages, many Jewish villages had a guest house where travelling beggars could stay for free.

Stained-glass detail of Abraham

Charity boxes are often seen in Jewish homes

Repairing the world

Loving your neighbour as yourself is an important part of Judaism. Each individual must be treated with the utmost respect and honour. Ignorance and intolerance darken the world, but love and understanding bring light and help to restore the world.

Hanukkah menorah *symbolizes the triumph of good over evil*

Charity

The Hebrew term *tzedakah* is used to describe charitable acts, and it is seen as the duty of every person to share what God has given them. Every week, before the start of *Shabbat*, people drop coins into a charity box, and on festivals such as *Purim*, collections are taken for various charities.

Torah scroll and *yad*

Education

The *Torah* stresses the importance of knowledge. Education is not only seen as a means of achieving a worthwhile career, but also as a way of teaching children how to behave correctly and be respectful to others.

Social responsibility

One of the commandments of Judaism is to look after others, just as God cared for Abraham when he was sick. The picture above shows friends visiting the biblical figure of Job, who had endured much suffering.

Kosher food

There are laws governing every aspect of Jewish life, including food laws (known as *kashrut*), which outline which foods can be eaten and how they should be prepared. The word *kosher* (meaning "fit" or "proper") is used to describe food that complies with these laws. Religious objects also have to be made in accordance with the rules. As well as being a biblical command, the food laws serve a hygienic function and help to preserve a sense of group identity.

The kosher shop
Many Jews buy their food from *kosher* shops. The majority of the packaged foods have a *kosher* label to show that a rabbi has visited the factory and that the food has been prepared correctly.

Meat and dairy
Animals that have cloven (split) hooves and chew the cud, such as lamb, are regarded as *kosher*, but pork is not. All animals have to be slaughtered by a trained person. Meat and dairy products cannot be eaten together and a household must have two sets of utensils and plates to keep meat and dairy products separate.

This kosher food stall only sells meat products. Such stalls are found in areas where there is a large Jewish community.

Parve food
Foods that are neither dairy nor meat are known as *parve* and can be eaten with both kinds of meals. These foods include fruit, vegetables, rice, eggs, and lentils.

Lentils

Crab

Seafood
Only fish with fins and scales, such as salmon, are *kosher*. Shellfish and other seafoods are not allowed. These forbidden foods are known as *treifah*.

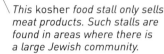

Salmon

Shofar

Religious objects
Religious objects such as the *shofar* have to be made from *kosher* animals. The parchment used for the *Torah* scroll also has to come from a *kosher* animal.

Passover
Certain ingredients cannot be eaten during Passover. For identification purposes, some food packages have a "*Kosher* for Passover" label, such as this box of *matzos*.

The kosher vineyard
The *Torah* instructs that grapes from a new vineyard cannot be used until the fourth year. Every seven years the vineyard has to be left fallow.

Wine production
Strict regulations apply to the production of *kosher* wine. The winery has a supervising rabbi to make sure that all the requirements have been met before issuing a *kosher* certificate.

Torah scroll

Kosher wine

The faces of Judaism

The majority of Jews today are descendants of the Ashkenazi (Eastern European) or the Sephardi (Spanish) Jews. There are several branches within these two main groups that differ in the strength of their beliefs, ranging from ultra-Orthodox to those adopting a more liberal approach. Various customs and traditions have developed in different Jewish communities around the world. Essentially, however, all Jews share a common history and language, no matter what customs they follow.

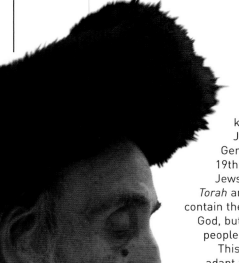

Conservative
Solomon Schechter (1847–1915) was the driving force behind the Conservative movement, which takes the middle ground between Orthodox and Reform Judaism.

Reform
The movement known as Reform Judaism began in Germany during the 19th century. Reform Jews believe that the *Torah* and *Talmud* do not contain the literal words of God, but were written by people inspired by God. This means they can adapt their faith to suit modern life, such as improving the status of Jewish women.

Female rabbi

Samaritan *Torah* scroll

An ultra-Orthodox Jew praying

Orthodox
Orthodox Jews follow traditional practices closely. The majority of Jews who live in Europe are Orthodox. But ultra-Orthodox Jews are one of the fastest-growing groups. These Jews tend to live in separate communities with their own schools and courts of law. Generally, they feel it is wrong to mix with the outside world, even with less-observant Jews.

Samaritans

The Samaritan community in Israel dates back to the 7th century BCE. Although they do not consider themselves to be Jews, they practise a form of Judaism. Samaritans accept the authority of the Five Books of Moses and observe the *Shabbat*.

Children in a *kibbutz* school, Israel

Jews in Israel

Israel is home to more than 6 million Jews, the second-largest community outside the USA. The Law of Return, which was passed by the Israeli government in 1950, allowed thousands of Jews to become citizens. Jews from countries throughout the world were all welcomed.

Ethiopian Jews

The existence of Ethiopian Jews, known as *Beta Israel* ("House of Israel"), only came to light during the 1850s. Their origin is a source of debate. Some Ethiopian Jews believe they are the descendants of the son of King Solomon and the Queen of Sheba. Others believe they belong to a lost tribe of Israel.

Ethiopian Jews take part in a blessing for Passover

Jews of India

The Jewish community of India was founded over 2,000 years ago. There were three groups: Bene Israel, the Cochin Jews, and those from European countries such as Spain. Today, there are only a few thousand Jews in India.

Copper plate granting privileges to a Jew, Joseph Rabban, dating from the 11th century, Cochin, India

Observant Yemenite Jews study the *Torah*

Yemenite Jews

There is evidence of Jews living in Yemen from the 1st century CE. Yemenite Jews have a very strong scholarly tradition and their own prayer book, called the *tiklal*.

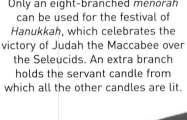

Symbols and language

Jewish communities now exist in every part of the world, and the people have preserved their way of life and faith. Over a period of time, the spoken Hebrew language declined, though it survived through religious use. Two symbols remain constant in representing the faith and identity of the Jewish people: the *menorah* (Hebrew for "candlestick") and the *Magen David*.

Hanukkah menorah

Only an eight-branched *menorah* can be used for the festival of *Hanukkah*, which celebrates the victory of Judah the Maccabee over the Seleucids. An extra branch holds the servant candle from which all the other candles are lit.

Seven-branched menorah

The seven-branched *menorah* is the oldest and most widely used symbol in Judaism. A gold *menorah* was kept in the Tabernacle and in the First and Second Temples.

The flag of Israel

The six points of the star represent the six days of creation

Blue represents heaven, and serves as a reminder of God's ways

White symbolizes purity and peace

Star of David

In Hebrew, the Star of David is known as the *Magen David*. The six-pointed star was first used as a decorative feature during the Roman period. It gained national significance when it was used for the First Zionist Congress in 1897. Since the creation of the State of Israel in 1948, the star has been used on the national flag.

Stone carving of the Star of David, dating from the 4th century CE

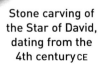

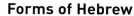
Eliezer
Ben-Yehuda

Ben-Yehuda

In the late 19th century there was a revival of spoken Hebrew. Eliezer Ben-Yehuda (1858–1922), decided to revive the language, which evolved into modern-day Hebrew. He published the first of his six-volume Hebrew dictionary in 1910.

Forms of Hebrew

The nature of ancient Hebrew changed when Jews settled in new countries. Jews who settled in Spain and Portugal in the Middle Ages spoke a form of Hebrew known as Ladino. In Eastern Europe, Yiddish was widely spoken until the 20th century.

Ancient Hebrew scroll

The seven branches represent the days of the week

The first ten letters of the Hebrew alphabet

The alphabet

A 22-letter alphabet was already being used when the Israelites settled in Canaan. When the Israelites were exiled in the 8th century BCE, Hebrew was written in a square script, which is still used today.

Language of Israel

Modern Hebrew is the official language of the State of Israel. Today, nearly four million Israelis speak it as their first language.

This Coca-Cola label is written in modern Hebrew

Written Hebrew

Hebrew is written from right to left. Children learn to read and write with the vowels, which are represented by little marks that surround the main script. Although most Jews speak the language of the country they live in, it is still important for them to be able to read Hebrew prayers in synagogue services.

Front cover of the *Jewish News*

Printed Hebrew

The 19th century saw the publication of Hebrew newspapers, adverts, and labels. The written form of Hebrew was no longer being used just for religious books.

Rites of passage

In Judaism, key life events are marked with special ceremonies. The circumcision of baby boys is a universal Jewish custom, dating back to biblical times. *Bar* and *Bat Mitzvah* mark the point at which children become adult members of the community. There are also specific Jewish customs marking marriage and death. All these rites of passage are celebrated publicly, stressing the communal nature of Jewish life.

Bar and Bat Mitzvah
The *Bar* and *Bat Mitzvah* celebrate adulthood and the taking on of religious responsibilities. This *siddur* is a typical *Bat Mitzvah* present.

Birth

In addition to an English name, every Jewish child is given a Hebrew name. The Hebrew name of a baby boy is announced at his *Brit Milah* (circumcision) ceremony, while that of a baby girl is announced in the synagogue on the first *Shabbat* after her birth or, alternatively, at a special baby-naming ceremony.

Circumcision ceremony
Brit Milah is carried out on the eighth day after the birth of a boy. It dates back to God's promise with Abraham that every male child be circumcised to show that he is a member of the Jewish people.

Paper amulet, Morocco, 20th century

Circumcision amulets
In former times, circumcision amulets (charms) were used by some communities to protect newborn babies against evil. These small pieces of parchment, paper, or metal were inscribed with magical signs and names of angels or of God. They were worn, or placed near the baby's cot.

Amulet from Germany,
19th century

Coming of Age

At the age of 13, a boy is considered to be *Bar Mitzvah* ("son of the commandment") and becomes responsible for his religious actions. He must fast on *Yom Kippur* and may be counted as part of the *minyan* in the synagogue. A girl is considered to be *Bat Mitzvah* ("daughter of the commandment") at the age of 12.

This woman wears a tallit and a kippa for her ceremony

Bat Mitzvah

Bat Mitzvah ceremonies for girls did not develop until the start of the 20th century. Today, this rite of passage is marked in different ways. In some communities, the girl reads from the *Torah*. In the Orthodox *Bat Chayil*, the girl gives a sermon in the synagogue. Some Orthodox communities do not publicly mark *Bat Mitzvah*.

Tefillin

An Orthodox boy will be given a set of *tefillin* for his *Bar Mitzvah*. When not being worn they are kept in a bag, which may be decorated with the boy's Hebrew name.

Tefillin case with the boy's name in Hebrew

Tefillin

A boy reads from the Torah *during a weekday ceremony*

Bar Mitzvah

At a *Bar Mitzvah* ceremony, the boy is called to read a section from the *Torah*, which he has prepared in advance. This symbolizes his acceptance of the commandments. The *Bar Mitzvah* is celebrated after the synagogue service, where most boys also give a speech called a *dvar Torah* ("word of *Torah*").

Continued on next page

The huppah *is depicted in this ancient* Torah *binder*

Marriage

Observant Jews see marriage as a gift from God, and it is an important religious occasion. Ceremonies vary depending on whether the service is Orthodox or Reform, and there are also different local customs. Generally, Jewish weddings can take place anywhere – in a synagogue, at home, or in the open air.

The ornate head-dress contains the herb rue to ward off evil

Breaking the glass

The end of the wedding ceremony is marked by the breaking of a wine glass. This symbolizes the destruction of the Temple and the fragility of marriage.

Dress

In many Jewish weddings, it is traditional for the bride (and sometimes the groom) to wear white. In contrast, Yemenite Jews dress in ornate clothing (left).

The huppah

The main service is conducted by a rabbi under a cloth canopy called a *huppah*. In some communities, a prayer shawl is held over the bride and groom. The *huppah* symbolizes the couple's new home.

The ketubah *is beautifully decorated with motifs*

The ketubah

The marriage contract, or *ketubah*, details the obligations of the groom towards his bride. It is signed by the groom at the start of the ceremony, although in modern weddings both the bride and groom sign the document.

Ornate Italian wedding ring

Wedding ring

In traditional Jewish weddings, the groom places a ring on the bride's finger and blessings are recited. In the past, some Jewish communities would lend the bride a magnificent ring, often decorated with a miniature house and inscribed with the words *Mazel Tov* ("Good Luck").

An old custom

Traditionally, a father would begin saving almost from the time his daughter was born so he could give her a dowry. In the case of orphans or girls from very poor families, the Jewish community would pool together to provide basic items for a dowry.

This necklace belonged to a Jewish bride from Bokhara, Uzbekistan, and dates from the 19th century

15th-century bridal casket, Italy

Bridal casket

In the past, the bride would be given gifts by the groom. The *ketubah* stated that if the couple divorced, the woman would be able to keep these possessions. This made Judaism an enlightened religion, because, for centuries, Christian or Muslim wives had no formal right to any property in the event of a divorce.

Death customs

The traditional customs associated with the last rite of passage have two purposes: to show respect for the dead and to help the grieving process. Mourners usually express their initial grief by making a tear in their clothing. It is also important for the deceased to be buried promptly (usually within three days). However, some Jews today prefer cremation.

Yahrzeit candle

Mark of respect

From the time of the death to the burial, the body is not left alone. A special candle is lit and placed next to the body as a sign of respect. On the eve of the anniversary another candle is lit, known as *yahrzeit* (meaning "year time").

An old Jewish cemetery in Worms, Germany

Mourning customs

A seven-day mourning period known as *shiva* begins on the day of the burial. All mirrors in the house are covered, and mourners sit on low stools, reciting the *kaddish*, a prayer in praise of God.

Shofar

High Holy Days

The themes of forgiveness and repentance are reflected in the most important holy days in Judaism – *Rosh Hashanah* (the Jewish New Year) and *Yom Kippur* (the Day of Atonement). These High Holy Days take place in September or October, depending on the Hebrew calendar. During this time, Jews think about the deeds of the past year and ask God for forgiveness.

Rosh Hashanah

This festival is seen as a time of judgement when God decides a person's fate for the coming year. His judgement is noted in one of three books: one for the good, one for the wicked, and one for the average person. During the next ten days, people are given a chance to repent, since God's final judgement is sealed at *Yom Kippur*.

The shofar

An important ritual associated with *Rosh Hashanah* is the sounding of the *shofar*. The instrument is often made from a ram's horn as a reminder of the ram sacrificed by Abraham. The sound of the *shofar* is intended to inspire people to reflect on the past year and resolve to lead a better life in the year to come.

Tashlikh

On *Rosh Hashanah*, many people go to a river or sea and throw breadcrumbs into the water to symbolize the casting off of sins. This custom is known as *tashlikh*.

A Happy New Year!

לְשָׁנָה טוֹבָה תִּכָּתֵבוּ!

Rosh Hashanah card

New Year customs
In some communities, people send New Year cards. Unlike secular (non-religious) New Year celebrations, this is a time for Jewish people to ask forgiveness from God and from those who have been wronged.

Kiwi fruit

Papaya

Honey

Apple

A sweet new year
On the eve of the festival it is customary to eat a piece of apple dipped in honey, or an exotic fruit, in the hope that the new year will be sweet.

Tzedakah (charity) box

Yom Kippur

The holiest day of the Jewish calendar is *Yom Kippur*. Apart from the sick, everyone above the age of *Bar* or *Bat Mitzvah* fasts for 25 hours, and most people spend the entire day praying in a synagogue to make amends with God. The service ends with a single blast of the *shofar*, and people leave with a new sense of purpose.

Jonah being cast into the sea for disobeying God

Giving to charity
The High Holy Day prayers say that those who sincerely repent, pray, and give to charity will be granted a good year. The rabbi will often encourage people to donate to a particular charity.

The Book of Jonah
On *Yom Kippur* the Book of Jonah is read in the synagogue. Jonah was asked by God to tell the people of Nineveh to repent. At first, he refused, but God forced him to deliver the message. God showed compassion by saving the people who repented.

Festivals

There are many important religious festivals throughout the Jewish year. These are celebrated not only in synagogues but also with rituals at home, each one marked with a different type of food. Each festival starts on the evening before the event and then continues on the next day, because in biblical times the day began at sunset.

The sukkah
The *sukkah* is a temporary shelter. It is built with three walls and a small gap left in the roof so that people can see the stars – a reminder that God is looking after them.

Sukkot

Etrog

Willow

Myrtle

The week-long festival of *Sukkot* (meaning "huts") is celebrated five days after the High Holy Days. *Sukkot* commemorates the time when the Israelites lived in temporary dwellings during the Exodus from Egypt. It also celebrates the gathering of the final harvest. A ritual associated with *Sukkot* is the blessing of the four plants known as the Four Species or *Lulav* – a palm branch, an etrog, myrtle, and willow.

Waving
During the service, the Four Species are waved in all directions to show that God is everywhere.

Palm branch

Blessings are recited on the Four Species

Decorating the sukkah
It is customary for children to help decorate the *sukkah* with pictures, paper chains, and seasonal fruit, representing the autumn harvest.

The procession
On each day of the festival a blessing is said while holding the Four Species. On the seventh day of *Sukkot*, followers end the morning service by walking around the synagogue seven times. The figure seven is symbolic of the seven processions made by the priests around the Temple in biblical times.

Simchat Torah

Immediately after *Sukkot* comes *Simchat Torah* ("rejoicing over the *Torah*"). The festival marks the end of the *Torah* readings and the start of a new cycle of readings. This shows that God's words are continuous. The *Torah* scrolls are taken out of the Ark and paraded outside the synagogue.

A Torah procession at the Western Wall, Israel

Sweets are given to children in the synagogue on Simchat Torah

The menorah

On each night of *Hanukkah*, the family gathers to light a candle. The *menorah* holds eight candles as well as a servant candle to light the others. By the end of the week, all eight candles are lit, symbolizing the miracle of the oil in the Temple.

Chocolate coins

Hanukkah traditions

During *Hanukkah*, people often eat food cooked in oil, such as *latkes* (potato cakes) to remember the miracle of the oil. In some communities, children receive chocolate coins.

Latkes

Hanukkah

The festival of *Hanukkah* commemorates an important historical event. Nearly 2,000 years ago, Jews in ancient Israel were not allowed to practise their faith. They rebelled against their rulers and won a monumental battle. The Jews relit the eternal lamp in the Temple, and although they only had enough oil to last one day, miraculously the oil lasted for eight days.

A candle is lit each night

The dreidel

As the candles burn, children play with a spinning top called a *dreidel*. On each side is a Hebrew letter standing for the words "a great miracle happened there".

Continued on next page

Continued from previous page

Olive branch

Tu Bishvat

Historically, 10 per cent of agricultural produce had to be given to priests and the poor on the festival of *Tu Bishvat*. In Israel today, the festival is seen as a time to plant new trees and for eating the fruits of the land.

Planting trees

Some children in Israel plant a sapling on *Tu Bishvat*, which falls in January. Jews in other communities are encouraged to sponsor a tree in Israel through the Jewish National Fund.

Purim

The festival of *Purim* is usually celebrated in March. Jews read the *Megillah* (Book of Esther), which recounts the story of Esther and Mordecai, who lived in Persia (now Iran) in the 5th century BCE. They devised a plan to stop a wicked court official, Haman, from killing Persian Jews.

The scroll

On the eve of *Purim*, and on the day itself, Jews go to the synagogue to read the Book of Esther. Unlike other biblical books, there is no mention of God in the *Megillah*.

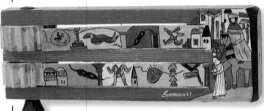

Gregger

The service

The synagogue service reflects the fun spirit of *Purim*. Whenever the name of Haman is mentioned, people hiss or shake *greggers* (rattles).

The story of Esther is handwritten on parchment

Esther   Mordecai

An 18th-century Persian *Megillah*

The parade

As well as listening to the *Megillah*, people eat a festive meal, exchange gifts of food, and give to charity. Some communities organize parties and parades at which colourful costumes are worn.

The annual *Purim* parade in Tel Aviv, Israel

Bitter herb

An egg reminds Jews of the sacrifices made in biblical times

Meat symbolizes the lamb sacrificed on the first Passover

Bitter herbs reflect the bitter experience of slavery

Green vegetables represent spring and new life

Charoset (a nut and fruit paste) is symbolic of the mortar used by Jewish slaves to build the cities

Passover

In March or April, Jews celebrate the festival of Passover (*Pesach* in Hebrew). Jews commemorate the time when Moses led the Israelites out of Egypt – this was the beginning of a Jewish nation. The family gathers to eat a celebratory meal called a *seder* (meaning "order") and sing songs of praise to God.

The Haggadah

Passover lasts for eight days, and on the first two nights the story of the Exodus is read from the *Haggadah*. A child present at the meal asks four questions and the questions are answered by retelling the story. The detail of the Passover meal shown below is from a medieval *Haggadah*.

The Passover table

The food on the *seder* plate (above) symbolizes the story of the Israelites in ancient Egypt. A glass of salt water is also placed on the table to represent the bitter tears of the enslaved Israelites.

Matzos

Unleavened bread

When the Israelites left Egypt in a hurry, the only food they could take was some bread that had not risen. Today, Jews refrain from eating any food that contains leaven (yeast) during Passover. *Matzo* is usually eaten instead of bread.

Continued on next page

Omer

In ancient Israel, the 49 days between Passover and the festival of *Shavuot* were counted. This period was known as the *Omer*. It marked the end of the barley harvest and the start of the wheat harvest. A sheaf of the new season's barley was offered at the Temple.

Lag BaOmer

Day 33 of the *Omer* calendar is known as *Lag BaOmer*. A noted *Torah* scholar called Rabbi Akiva lost 24,000 of his students in an epidemic during the *Omer* period. However, on the *Lag BaOmer*, no one died. Some Jews light bonfires to mark the occasion.

Omer calendar

Some Jews still count down the days between Passover and *Shavuot* using a special calendar.

Omer calendar for children

Seven species

As well as the commandments, *Shavuot* celebrates the bringing of the first fruits (shown below) to the Temple in Jerusalem.

Barley

Dates

Grapes

Wheat

Figs

Olives

Pomegranates

Shavuot

The Greek name for the two-day festival of *Shavuot* is *Pentecost*, from the word for "fifty", because it begins after the 49 days of *Omer*. *Shavuot* celebrates the giving of the *Torah* by God to Moses on Mount Sinai and the start of the new wheat harvest. During the synagogue service, the Book of Ruth and the Ten Commandments are read.

Children in a kibbutz school celebrate Shavuot *as a harvest festival*

Traditions

On *Shavuot*, synagogues are decorated with flowers to celebrate the giving of the commandments. Some people eat dairy foods to recall the time when the Israelites ate only dairy food while waiting to hear the commandments.

Shabbat

The Jewish day of rest, the Sabbath is known in Hebrew as the *Shabbat*. It begins every Friday at sunset with the lighting of the *Shabbat* candles and ends the following Saturday night.

Cup for washing hands

Washing hands
Before the *Shabbat* meal, some Jews wash their hands three times with a special two-handed cup.

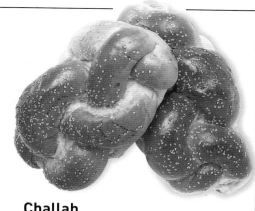

Challah
The two *challah* loaves on the *Shabbat* table recall the time when the Israelites wandered in the desert. God gave them manna to eat every day, but on Friday they received double the amount.

"Remember the Sabbath day and keep it holy. On the seventh day you shall do no work."

ONE OF THE TEN COMMANDMENTS

Shabbat table

Wicks symbolize the unity of the Jewish people

Havdalah
The ceremony marking the end of *Shabbat* is called *havdalah*, which means "separation". It features a plaited candle (left), wine, and sweet-smelling spices (right).

Havdalah candle

Spice box used on *Shabbat*

The meaning of Shabbat
Just as God rested on the seventh day after creating the world, observant Jews do not work at all on *Shabbat*. It is traditional to invite guests home for the *Shabbat* evening meal, especially those without families. Essentially, *Shabbat* is seen as a time to worship, rest, and be with the community.

Plaited candle
The *havdalah* candle recalls the light created by God when he brought order to the world.

Jewish contribution

Despite the prejudice and hostility faced by Jews over the years, their contribution to all aspects of life has been remarkable. The Jewish people have felt motivated to make their mark – from the lasting legacy of music and art, to pioneering discoveries in science and medicine. Many Jews have become involved in politics, driven by a desire to create a more tolerant and peaceful world.

The arts

Jews have enriched the world through their passion for music, drama, painting, literature, and design. A combination of drive and imagination has kept them at the forefront of the arts. For example, immigrants to the USA almost single-handedly set up the early film studios in Hollywood – including 20th Century Fox, Metro-Goldwyn-Mayer, and Warner Brothers.

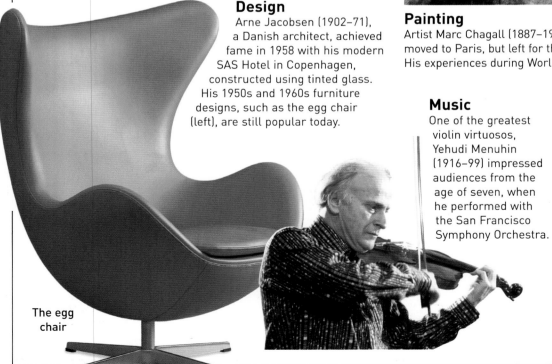

Design
Arne Jacobsen (1902–71), a Danish architect, achieved fame in 1958 with his modern SAS Hotel in Copenhagen, constructed using tinted glass. His 1950s and 1960s furniture designs, such as the egg chair (left), are still popular today.

The egg chair

Painting
Artist Marc Chagall (1887–1985) was born in Russia. In 1910, he moved to Paris, but left for the USA following German occupation. His experiences during World War II had a huge impact on his work.

Music
One of the greatest violin virtuosos, Yehudi Menuhin (1916–99) impressed audiences from the age of seven, when he performed with the San Francisco Symphony Orchestra.

Literature of the mind
Sigmund Freud (1856–1939) studied medicine in Austria, and went on to develop a new science of the mind – psychoanalysis. He moved to England in 1938 to escape the Nazi occupation.

Community by Marc Chagall

Film poster for *Schindler's List* (1993)

Film-making
Film director Steven Spielberg gave millions of people their first insight into the horrors of the Holocaust with his film *Schindler's List*.

Politics

A history of a people in turmoil, together with the Jewish teaching that demands concern for the less fortunate, has led many Jews to become involved in politics and peace-making.

US President Bill Clinton witnesses the historic handshake in 1993

Yitzhak Rabin

Diplomacy
Henry Kissinger (b. 1923) was a refugee from Nazi Germany who went on to become the US Secretary of State. In 1972, he organized President Nixon's historic visits to Russia and China.

Peace-makers
In 1995, the Prime Minister of Israel, Yitzhak Rabin (1922–95), jointly won the Nobel Peace Prize for his part in the Israeli-Arab peace process. However, some people opposed his ideas, and, in 1995, he was assassinated at a peace rally in Tel Aviv, Israel.

Yasser Arafat, joint winner of the Nobel Peace Prize

Continued on next page

The pioneers

Jewish pioneers have influenced many areas of our lives – from the clothes we wear to the way we travel. Often facing prejudice in established industries, Jews have been at the forefront of developing new technologies that have improved the lives of millions of people.

Levi's denim jeans

Aviation design
Emile Berliner (1851–1929) was a prolific inventor. In 1919, he developed a prototype helicopter.

Clothes design
Born in Germany, Levi Strauss (1829–1902) moved to California, USA. After hearing gold miners complain that their trousers wore out too quickly, he made them jeans with metal rivets on the pockets. The hard-wearing item became a global success.

Helena Rubenstein highlights the basic contours of the face

Beauty specialist
Polish-born Helena Rubenstein (1870–1965) revolutionized the beauty industry with her medicated face creams. In 1953, she set up the Helena Rubenstein Foundation, caring for needy women and children.

The classic Olivetti M-40 typewriter

Office technology
Italian activist Adriano Olivetti (1901–60) built his father's typewriter company into the largest manufacturer of business machines in Europe. During World War II, the Olivetti factory became headquarters for the resistance movement.

Industrial engineering
The son of a gem merchant from Poland, French industrialist André Citroën (1878–1935) designed a range of affordable cars for the French working man.

Citroën Traction Avant

Henry Berliner, Emile's son, makes a test flight in the new American "chopper"

Berliner's flying machine had a rotating blade that lifted it straight up into the air

Science and medicine

The Jewish contribution to science and medical care has been monumental. In medicine, Jews have been responsible for discovering vaccines to combat many killer diseases, including cholera, bubonic plague, typhoid fever, and polio.

Cluster of polio viruses

Physics

One of the world's greatest scientists, Albert Einstein (1879–1955) devised the theory of relativity, which changed the way people viewed the world. In 1921, he was awarded the Nobel Prize for Physics. Born in Germany, Einstein moved to Switzerland as a young man. When the Nazis came to power, he settled in the USA.

Paul Ehrlich, bacteriologist, at work in his laboratory

Medical science

German-born Paul Ehrlich (1854–1915) developed the idea of the "magic bullet" – a drug that would only attack the diseased parts of the body without damaging healthy cells and tissues.

The fight to cure polio

Jonas Salk (1914–95), the son of Russian immigrants, developed the first polio vaccine to fight the disease that killed thousands. His vaccine was administered by injection. However, it was Polish American Albert Sabin (1906–93) who developed the oral vaccine approved for worldwide use.

People and places in the Bible

ABRAHAM
The first patriarch of the nation of Israel, Abraham entered into a covenant with God, who led him to the land of Canaan.

ADAM
The first man, created by God.

BABYLON
City situated in the south of modern-day Baghdad in Iraq, and the capital of the Babylonian empire. In 587 BCE, King Nebuchadnezzar II of Babylon sacked Jerusalem, and the people of Judah were carried into exile.

BETHLEHEM
City in the Judean hills south of Jerusalem. The birthplace of David, chosen by the prophet Samuel to succeed Saul as king.

CAIN
Eldest son of Adam and Eve. When God accepted his brother Abel's sacrifice and rejected Cain's, Cain killed Abel.

CANAAN
The land promised to the Israelites by God.

CYRUS THE GREAT
King of Persia c.559–529 BCE who overthrew the Babylonians and allowed the Jews to return from their exile and rebuild the Temple in Jerusalem.

Abraham

DANIEL
Taken captive to Babylon c.605 BCE, Daniel interpreted King Nebuchadnezzar's dreams. Punished for his devotion to God, he was cast into a lions' den and survived.

DAVID
Shepherd boy from Bethlehem who killed Goliath. He became Israel's second king c.1010–970 BCE and founded the royal line from which the Messiah was to be born.

EGYPT
A major civilization from the third millennium BCE, and the setting for several biblical events, among them the stories of Joseph, Moses, and the Exodus.

ELIJAH
One of Israel's greatest prophets, who lived during the reign of King Ahab.

ESTHER
Jewish exile who married the Persian King Ahasuerus. When the wicked Haman persuaded the king that all Jews were traitors and must die, Esther revealed that she too was Jewish and begged the king to spare her people. The festival of *Purim* celebrates her heroism.

EVE
The first woman, created by God.

EZEKIEL
Major prophet who lived in Babylon during the exile. He denounced the sins of God's people and foretold the ruin of Jerusalem.

EZRA
Priest and scribe who returned to Jerusalem from Babylon with a company of exiles. Ezra read the laws of God to the people when the Temple was rebuilt.

GIDEON
A Judge of Israel. Gideon cut down monuments to false gods and led a tiny army of 300 men who defeated the Midianites.

Gideon

HEBRON
A town in the Judean hills, where Abraham camped, and David had his capital before he captured Jerusalem. Hebron was the traditional burial place of the patriarchs.

Nile River, Egypt

ISAAC
Son of Abraham and Sarah and one of the great patriarchs of Judaism.

ISAIAH
Major Judean prophet who lived during the Assyrian conquest of Judah in the 8th–7th century BCE.

ISRAEL
Land occupied by the 12 tribes. After the reign of Solomon, it was divided into two kingdoms: Israel in the north and Judah in the south.

JACOB
One of the great patriarchs of Judaism. Jacob cheated his brother Esau to win their father Isaac's blessing, and went to work for his uncle Laban, marrying Leah and Rachel. They bore him 12 sons, who founded the 12 tribes of Israel.

JEREMIAH
A prophet during the Babylonian exile who warned the Israelites not to forsake God.

JERICHO
Town west of the Jordan River. When the Israelites fought to win the Promised Land, God told Joshua to have the army to walk around the fortified city seven times, and the people shout to the skies, upon which the walls of Jericho fell.

JERUSALEM
The capital of the early kings of Israel and later of the southern kingdom of Judah. David brought the Ark of the Covenant here, making Jerusalem his capital, and it was here that his son Solomon built the First Temple. From that time on Jerusalem became the holy city for Jews.

JORDAN RIVER
Israel's main river. Joshua led the Israelites across the Jordan into the Promised Land.

JOSEPH
Jacob's favourite son. His jealous brothers sold him into slavery, but he rose to power in Egypt. Joseph was reunited with his brothers when they came to Egypt in search of food.

JOSHUA
After Moses died, Joshua led the Israelites into Canaan and divided the Promised Land among the 12 tribes of Israel.

JUDAH
The land belonging to the tribe of Judah, son of Jacob. When Israel was divided, Judah became the southern kingdom, with Jerusalem as its capital.

MOSES
Great leader and prophet. Born in Egypt, Moses led the Exodus to the Promised Land. Journeying for 40 years in the wilderness, he received the two

The Western Wall, Jerusalem

tablets of stone inscribed with the Ten Commandments on Mount Sinai, but died before he could enter Canaan.

NEBUCHADNEZZAR
King of Babylon who captured Jerusalem in 597 BCE and took the Judeans into exile.

NEHEMIAH
Cup-bearer to the Persian king, who returned to Jerusalem and organized the rebuilding of the city walls.

NOAH
Godly man in a time of great evil, who was told by God to build an ark and saved the animals from the Flood that destroyed the rest of humanity.

RACHEL
The wife of Jacob and mother of Joseph and Benjamin. In order to marry her, Jacob worked for seven years without pay.

REBEKAH
Wife of Isaac, and mother of Esau and Jacob. Jacob, the younger brother, was her favourite, and she tricked Isaac into blessing him instead of Esau.

Rebekah

RUTH
The widow from Moab, who dutifully escorted her mother-in-law to Bethlehem and worked hard during the harvest to provide for her.

SAMSON
Champion of Israel against the Philistines in the time of the Judges, until his wife Delilah robbed him of his strength by cutting his long hair as he slept.

SAMUEL
Priest, prophet, and leader who anointed Israel's first two kings, Saul and David.

SARAH
Wife of Abraham. Sarah was childless until old age, when she gave birth to Isaac. When she died, Abraham bought a cave near Hebron as her tomb.

SAUL
First king of Israel, c.1050–1010 BCE. Anointed by Samuel, Saul disobeyed God's command on three occasions and became jealous of the young David. Defeated by the Philistines, Saul fell on his sword.

SINAI
Mountain in the Sinai desert. During the Exodus, Moses received the Ten Commandments here.

SOLOMON
Son of David and Bathsheba, and the third king of Israel c.970–930 BCE. A key figure in the history of Judaism, he built the First Temple, and his wisdom was legendary: he passed judgement on two women who claimed to be the mother of the same baby.

TEMPLE MOUNT
The hill in Jerusalem on which David founded his capital city and Solomon built the First Temple. Today, the Dome of the Rock sits on top of the site that is sacred to Muslims and Jews.

Samson

The Jewish calendar

Jewish years are counted from the first *Shabbat* of Creation. While Judaism traditionally dates Creation to 3760 BCE, Reform and many Orthodox Jews today accept that the world is far older. The annual festivals of Judaism mark the agricultural seasons and commemorate major events of the past.

The day begins
In biblical times, sunset signalled the end of one day and the beginning of the next. In the Jewish calendar, each day of the week still begins at sunset the day before. *Shabbat*, the last day of the week, begins with the lighting of the *Shabbat* candles at sunset on Friday, and ends with the *havdalah* ceremony at nightfall on Saturday.

Major holidays
For ancient Israelites, time was dominated by agricultural seasons and historical events that are still marked by religious festivals today. The festivals begin in the autumn with the High Holy Days of *Rosh Hashanah* (the Jewish New Year) and *Yom Kippur* (the Day of Atonement).

Shabbat candles   *Havdalah* candle

Days of the week
In the Jewish calendar, only the seventh day of the week has a name – *Shabbat* – while the first six days of the week are merely numbered.
Sunday – *Yom Rishon* ("first day")
Monday – *Yom Sheini* ("second day")
Tuesday – *Yom Shlishi* ("third day")
Wednesday – *Yom Revi'i* ("fourth day")
Thursday – *Yom Chamishi* ("fifth day")
Friday – *Yom Shishi* ("sixth day")
Saturday – *Shabbat* ("Sabbath day")

September

August

July

June

May

Elul
(29 days)

Av
(30 days)

Tamuz
(29 days)

Sivan
(30 days)

Iyyar
(29 days)

Tisha B'av

Roman soldiers loot and burn the Temple

Ten Commandments

Shavuot

Count of the Omer

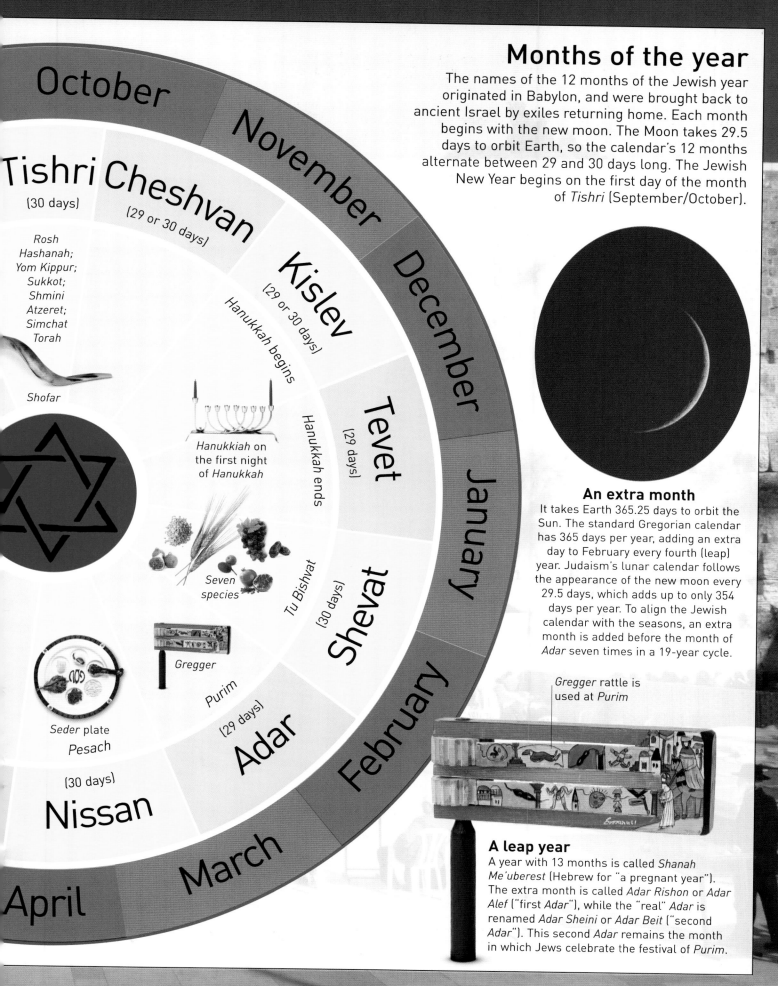

Months of the year

The names of the 12 months of the Jewish year originated in Babylon, and were brought back to ancient Israel by exiles returning home. Each month begins with the new moon. The Moon takes 29.5 days to orbit Earth, so the calendar's 12 months alternate between 29 and 30 days long. The Jewish New Year begins on the first day of the month of *Tishri* (September/October).

An extra month

It takes Earth 365.25 days to orbit the Sun. The standard Gregorian calendar has 365 days per year, adding an extra day to February every fourth (leap) year. Judaism's lunar calendar follows the appearance of the new moon every 29.5 days, which adds up to only 354 days per year. To align the Jewish calendar with the seasons, an extra month is added before the month of *Adar* seven times in a 19-year cycle.

Gregger rattle is used at *Purim*

A leap year

A year with 13 months is called *Shanah Me'uberest* (Hebrew for "a pregnant year"). The extra month is called *Adar Rishon* or *Adar Alef* ("first *Adar*"), while the "real" *Adar* is renamed *Adar Sheini* or *Adar Beit* ("second *Adar*"). This second *Adar* remains the month in which Jews celebrate the festival of *Purim*.

Calendar wheel

October

November

December

January

February

March

April

Tishri
(30 days)

Cheshvan
(29 or 30 days)

Kislev
(29 or 30 days)

Tevet
(29 days)

Shevat
(30 days)

Adar
(29 days)

Nissan
(30 days)

Rosh Hashanah;
Yom Kippur;
Sukkot;
Shmini Atzeret;
Simchat Torah

Shofar

Hanukkah begins

Hanukkiah on the first night of Hanukkah

Hanukkah ends

Seven species

Tu Bishvat

Gregger

Purim

Seder plate
Pesach

Find out more

David, in Florence, Italy

Whether or not you live in a big city with a bustling Jewish district, there are plenty of opportunities to learn about Judaism. Museums around the world trace the story of the Diaspora, and the terrible events of the Holocaust are commemorated by books, films, and survivors' accounts.

Look for Bible stories

In many art galleries round the world, you will find depictions of famous people and events from the Bible. The story of David and Goliath, for example, has inspired many masterpieces – not least Michelangelo's towering statue of David, created in 1501–04.

Visit a synagogue

Find out if your local synagogue welcomes visitors and arrange for a tour – remember to ask how you should dress as it is a place of worship. The magnificent 1887 Eldridge Street Synagogue in New York City was one of the first synagogues built in the USA by Jewish immigrants from Eastern Europe. Now restored, it still functions as a synagogue, while also housing a museum with guided tours and exhibitions about the history of American Jews and immigration.

Take a museum tour

The Jewish Museum in Rome, Italy, tells the story of one of the oldest Jewish communities in the world, dating back more than 2,000 years. Jewish museums all over the world celebrate the history, traditions, and culture of Judaism, and provide information on the Diaspora and the Holocaust.

Concrete slabs resemble rows of tombstones in a cemetery

Remember the Holocaust

Visit a Holocaust memorial or exhibition in your area, and check what local and national events mark the annual Holocaust Memorial Day on 27 January. In Berlin, Germany, visitors can walk among the 2,711 funerary slabs at the Memorial to the Murdered Jews of Europe.

PLACES TO VISIT

JEWISH MUSEUM LONDON, UNITED KINGDOM

Among its exhibitions are the Welcome Gallery, featuring 10 very different accounts of what it is like to be Jewish in Britain today. There are also treasures from London's Great Synagogue, which was burnt down in 1941.

UNITED STATES HOLOCAUST MEMORIAL MUSEUM, WASHINGTON DC, USA

One of the most important Holocaust museums in the world, this museum has a wide range of artefacts and exhibitions. There are moving eyewitness accounts and over 100,000 historical photographs and images, including Daniel's Story – an exhibition for children over eight, which tells the tale of the Holocaust from the viewpoint of one German-Jewish boy.

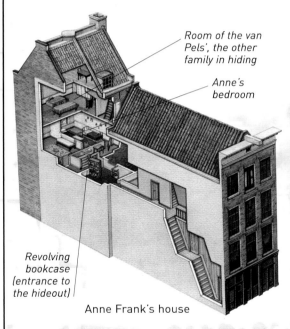

Room of the van Pels', the other family in hiding

Anne's bedroom

Revolving bookcase (entrance to the hideout)

Anne Frank's house

Step into the past

In many cities across Europe and beyond, thriving Jewish districts maintain the traditions of the past. Behind the Old Town Square in Prague, Czech Republic, lies the historic Jewish Quarter dating back to the 10th century. The Marais district in Paris, France, is famous for its Jewish restaurants, bakeries, and bookshops.

Jewish bakery in Paris, France

ANNE FRANK HOUSE, AMSTERDAM, HOLLAND

The Anne Frank House gives a glimpse into the two years the Frank family spent in hiding during World War II. Visitors can see the annexe where Anne lived, as well as original documents detailing the story of the Frank family and photos of the famous diarist.

JEWISH MUSEUM ROME, ITALY

Located in the Great Synagogue of Rome, this museum includes a range of interactive features, such as a 3D virtual experience of life in a Jewish ghetto.

THE WESTERN WALL, JERUSALEM, ISRAEL

The only remaining outer wall of the Second Temple, this site is sacred for Jews, but can be visited by those of any religion.

Learn about Auschwitz

The Auschwitz-Birkenau Memorial and Museum in Poland confronts visitors with the stark realities of concentration and extermination camps. More than one million men, women, and children lost their lives here. Visits to the museum are not recommended for children under 14.

Entrance to Auschwitz I

Glossary

ANTI-SEMITISM
Prejudice against Jews that can lead to discrimination and persecution.

ARK
In a synagogue, a special cupboard in which the *Torah* scrolls are kept.

ARK OF THE COVENANT
The wooden chest that held the two stone tablets of the Ten Commandments during the Exodus. The Ark of the Covenant was later housed in the Temple in Jerusalem.

BAR MITZVAH
A ceremony when a 13-year-old boy becomes becomes an adult member of the Jewish community.

Ark of the Covenant

BAT MITZVAH
A ceremony when a 12-year-old girl becomes an adult member of the Jewish community.

BRIT MILAH
The Jewish circumcision ceremony that is a sign of God's promise with Abraham.

CIRCUMCISION
Removal of the foreskin. In Judaism, this usually takes place when a boy is eight days old, to show that he is a member of the Jewish people.

COVENANT
A binding agreement. In the Bible, God makes a series of covenants with His people: for example, with Noah after the Flood, with Moses on Mount Sinai, and with King David.

DAY OF ATONEMENT
Yom Kippur, the holiest day in the Jewish year, marked by fasting and prayers.

Bar Mitzvah

DIASPORA
(Greek for "scattering") The dispersal of large groups of Jews across the world.

EXILE
Banishment from one's homeland. Many of the inhabitants of Israel and Judah were deported by foreign conquerors.

EXODUS
(Greek for "way out") The Israelites' departure from Egypt, led by Moses.

FASTING
Abstaining from food and water.

GHETTO
The restricted part of a city in which a minority group is made to live, segregated from other people.

HAGGADAH
(Hebrew for "the telling") The book that recounts the story of the Exodus.

HEBREW
The language of the Jewish Bible, of the Israelites, and of modern-day Israel.

HOLOCAUST
The mass murder of six million Jews and other groups by the Nazis during World War II.

ISRAEL
In the Bible, the name given to Jacob, and to the nation of 12 tribes that became two kingdoms – Israel and Judah. The modern state of Israel was founded in 1948.

KASHRUT
Judaism's dietary laws, outlining which foods can be eaten and how they should be prepared.

KETUVIM
The third part of the Hebrew Bible: the Psalms, the Proverbs, and the Song of Songs.

KIBBUTZ
A collective settlement in Israel – often a farm that is worked by members who receive no pay but share everything.

KIPPA
A head covering worn by male Jews as a sign of respect in God's constant presence.

KOSHER
Used to describe animals and foods that comply with Jewish dietary laws.

Text in Hebrew (top), Arabic, and English

MENORAH
The seven-branched candlestick used in the Tabernacle and in the Temple; subsequently a symbol of Judaism. The *menorah* used during *Hanukkah* has eight candles and a servant candle to light all the others.

MESSIAH
In the Bible, a king or high priest chosen by God to lead his people. For Jews, the Messiah has yet to come.

MEZUZAH
A small piece of parchment inscribed with the *Shema* prayer and placed in a container (also known as a *mezuzah*).

MIDRASH
(Hebrew for "to search") The collection of commentaries by rabbis seeking to help explain the *Torah*.

MINYAN
A prayer group of at least 10 people.

MITZVOT
The commandments in the *Torah*.

MYSTICAL
Inspiring a sense of spiritual mystery. The *Kabbalah*'s mystical teachings present an alternative view of the world in their analysis of the *Torah*.

NEVI'IM
The writings of the Prophets, forming the second part of the Hebrew Bible.

NOMADIC
Travelling from place to place in search of water and fresh pasture for livestock.

OBSERVANCE
The act of practising (following) a religion – obeying its rules, complying with its customs, and attending its ceremonies.

ORTHODOX
(Greek for "correct belief") Following a core set of traditional beliefs or rules. Orthodox Jews believe the *Torah* was dictated by God to Moses.

PALESTINE
The land between the Jordan River and the Mediterranean. In the Bible, it is also referred to as Canaan, the Promised Land, or the Land of Israel.

PASSOVER
The annual festival of *Pesach*, commemorating the Exodus.

PATRIARCH
The male head of a family or tribe. Also used of Israelite leaders before the time of Moses – in particular, Abraham, Isaac, and Jacob.

POGROM
(Russian for "devastation") Violent destruction of a Jewish community.

PROMISED LAND
Canaan, the land between the Jordan River and the Mediterranean Sea, promised by God to Abraham.

PROPHET
Someone through whom God speaks in the Bible.

RABBI
(Hebrew for "master" or "teacher") A Jewish religious teacher and spiritual leader. Hence the term "Rabbinic", relating to rabbis, their teachings, or their writings.

Rabbi

SABBATH
See *Shabbat*.

SACRIFICE
An offering made to God, particularly a living animal.

SCRIPTURES
The Bible for Jews and Christians. Also any book of writings considered to be sacred.

SECT
A branch or subgroup within a religion, following a distinct set of beliefs or rituals. In Judaism, the major sects are Orthodox, Reform, and Conservative.

SECULAR
Not observing religious laws or following a religious way of life.

Seder plate

SEDER
A celebratory meal eaten during the annual festival of Passover.

SHABBAT
(Hebrew for "Sabbath") The seventh day of the week, set aside as a day of rest and worship, beginning at sunset on Friday and finishing on Saturday evening.

SHEMA
(Hebrew for "Hear") An important daily prayer that declares the oneness and supremacy of God.

SHOFAR
A ram's horn that is blown on High Holy Days.

SHTETL
A small, mainly Jewish village or town.

SIDDUR
A Jewish book of daily prayers.

STAR OF DAVID
A symbol of Judaism known in Hebrew as the *Magen David*.

SYNAGOGUE
(Greek for "gathering") A building in which Jews meet for worship and study.

TABERNACLE
The large portable tent in which the Israelites carried the Ark of the Covenant during the Exodus from Egypt to Canaan.

TALMUD
(Hebrew for "study") An extensive Jewish religious work containing interpretations of, and commentaries on, the *Torah*.

TALLIT
A prayer shawl.

TEFELLIN
Two black leather boxes containing words from the *Torah*, worn during prayer.

TEMPLE
The ancient Jewish Temple in Jerusalem. The First Temple was built by Solomon and destroyed by the Babylonians. The Second Temple was extensively rebuilt by Herod the Great, and destroyed by the Romans in 70 CE.

TEN COMMANDMENTS
In Judaism, these are the first of 613 *mitzvot* (commandments) given by God to Moses. They form the basis of Jewish ethics and behaviour.

TORAH
(Hebrew for "teaching" or "direction") Judaism's holiest teachings, also known as the Five Books of Moses: Genesis, Exodus, Leviticus, Numbers, and Deuteronomy. These form the first part of the Hebrew Bible.

TZEDAKAH
Charity. In Judaism, giving aid is an important act of duty and justice.

UNLEAVENED
Made from dough containing no yeast (leaven).

YAD
(Hebrew for "hand") The pointer used to follow the text while reading the *Torah*.

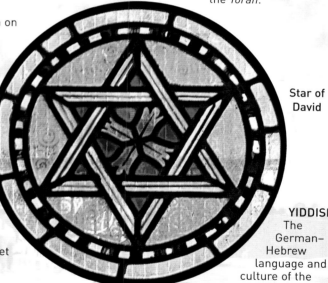

Star of David

YIDDISH
The German–Hebrew language and culture of the world's Ashkenazi Jews, who originated from Central and Eastern Europe.

ZION
Originally the south-eastern hill of Jerusalem, which became known as the "City of David". It was here that King Solomon built the First Temple. The term Zion became an alternative name in the Bible for the city of Jerusalem and for the Land of Israel and its people.

ZIONISM
The political movement for the creation of a Jewish state in Palestine.

Index

Acknowledgements

Dorling Kindersley would like to thank: Steimatzky and Jerusalem the Golden for their generosity
Design assistance: Sheila Collins
Editorial assistance: Fran Jones, Sadie Smith, Clare Lister, and Zahavit Shalev
Index: Hilary Bird
Authoring text: Camilla Hallinan
Text editing: Hazel Beynon
Proofreading: Chris Hawkes

The publisher would like to thank the following for their kind permission to reproduce their photographs:

Picture credits:
a-above; b-(below; c-centre; l-left; r-right; t-top

123RF.com: anyka 71cl, Felix Lipov 70bc. **AKG London:** 9tl, 15c, 18c, 26b, 27tr, 29c, 41cbr; Erich Lessing 58tr; Stefan Diller 19l. **Ancient Art & Architecture Collection:** 14cr, 16b, 40bl. **Arcaid:** Alan Weintraub 33cl. **The Art Archive:** Biblioteca Nacional Lisbon/Dagli Orti 53br; Bibliothèque des Arts Decoratifs Paris/Dagli Orti 9cb; Dagli Orti 10cl; Israel Museum Jerusalem/Dagli Orti 1c; Museuo Capitolino Rome/Dagli Orti 17br; Nationalmuseet Copenhagen Denmark/Dagli Orti (A) 19br. **Art Directors & TRIP:** Ask Images 48tr; H Rogers 39tl,

47br; I. Genut 40c; S. Shaprio 54tr. **Art Resource:** The Jewish Museum, New York 56c. **Rabbi Eliezer Ben-Yehuda:** 47tl. **Werner Braun:** 52br, 55tc, 56b. **Bridgeman Art Library, London/New York:** Basilica di San Marco, Venice, Italy 8tr; Bibliothèque Nationale, Paris 12bl; Bibliothèque Nationale, Paris, France 18br; British Library, London 13c; Giraudon 38tl; Lauros/Giraudon 57br; Musee de la Revolution Francaise, Vizille, France 21tl; Private Collection 20cr, 39br. **British Library:** 47tl. **British Museum:** 8cl, 8c. **Camera Press:** 29cb, 29br. **Citroën UK Ltd:** 62b. **Coca-Cola Company:** 47bl. **Corbis:** 60br; Araldo de Luca 62cr; Archivo Iconografico, S.A 6tl, 6cr, 15tr; Atlantide Phototravel 69cl; Barry Lewis 32bl; Bettmann 22bl, 28c, 28bl, 31cl, 62–63cr, 63cl, 63b; Burstein Collection 60–61cr; Dean Conger 8–9b, 11tr; Gianni Dagli Orti 10b, 14tl; Hayan Isachar 54b; Leonard de Selva 24cl; Lizzie Shepherd / Design Pics 64b; Moshe Shai 58tl; Nathan Benn 17cl; Paul A. Souders 34br; Peter M. Wilson 38bl; Peter Turnley 44cc; Rabbi Naamah Kelman 44cc; Richard T. Nowitz 6b, 14b, 32tr, 58br; Shai Ginott 46br; Stapleton Collection 36tr; Ted Spiegel 31bc; Unger Kevin/Sygma 45cra; West Semitic Research/Dead Sea Scrolls Foundation 37tc. **Dorling Kindersley:** Barnabas

Kindersley 64tr; Fleur Star 43tl. **Dreamstime.com:** Alexirina27000 66cr; David Murray 70cr; Dennis Van De Water 67tr; Hel080808 68crb; Sean Pavone 68c. **E & E Picture Library:** 59b. **Mary Evans Picture Library:** 12tl, 18tl, 24bl, 26tl, 26c, 27tl, 27cl, 53tl; Cassell, Petter & Galpin 22tr; Explorer Archives 40tl; Weimar Archive 31t. **Moshe Frumin:** 12br. **Getty Images:** Giorgio Cosulich 68cra. **Glasgow Museum:** 2c, 4bcl, 52tl. **Golders Green United Synagogue:** 4l, 54l. **Ronald Grant Archive:** 60bc. **Fritz Hansen A/S:** 60bl. **Robert Harding Picture Library:** E. Simanor 43b; M. F. Chillmaid 19tr. **Beth Hatefutsoth, Photo Archive, Tel Aviv:** 18bl, 25tr, 32cr, 44tl; Central Zionist Archives, Jerusalem 22cl, 24tr, 25br, 25c; Courtesy of E. M. Stern 45cb; Ghetto Fighter's House-Photo Archive 30c; Jewish National and University Library, Jerusalem 39tr; Municipal Archives of Rome 20tr; Tel Aviv, The Gross Family Collection 24br. **Heritage Image Partnership:** British Museum 13tr; The British Museum 14cl. **© Michael Holford:** 9r. **Hulton Archive/ Getty Images:** 22–23bc, 23cr, 26tr, 27br, 29tl, 29cr, 30bl, 62cl; Leo Baeck Inst. NYC. Photo Gemeinden Deutschland. Macdonald and Co. 27cb. **Hutchison Library:** J. Horner 42cr. **Impact Photos:** Stewart Weir 47bcr. **Imperial War Museum:** 28tl, 28br; James Johnson 30tl, 30cla. **Israelimages.com:** Avi Hirschfield 7bl; Israel Talby 32br, 45t; Richard Nowitz 46cb. **Israel Museum Jerusalem:** 11l, 16tl,

38–39bc, 48bl; D. Harris 48c; David Harris 51tr, 51cl. **Oscar Israelowitz:** 33tr. **Jewish Education Bureau:** 50cla. **Jewish Museum, London:** 2cr, 3c, 5tr, 16cl, 40-41cr, 50tl. **Joods Historisch Museum:** 20bl. **Kobal Collection:** 61tr. **Levi Strauss & Co:** 62tr. **Christine Osborne:** 56tc. **Popperfoto:** REUTERS 61bc. **Zev Radovan, Jerusalem:** 11cr, 11br, 12tr, 13cl, 15tl, 15tc, 15br, 16c, 17bl, 17r, 20tl, 37cl, 37br, 44bl, 44-45bc, 45br, 49tr, 49b, 50bc, 54cr. **Rex Features:** London Weekend 60bc; SIPA Press 61bl. **Anat Rotem, Jerusalem:** 7t. **Science Photo Library:** CDC 63cr. **Topham Picturepoint:** 29bc. **JerryYoung:** 42bl.

Wallchart: 123RF.com: serge75 tr. AKG London: cb (camp). Ancient Art & Architecture Collection: tl. The Art Archive: Bibliothèque des Arts Decoratifsb Paris/Dagli Orti cla. Bridgeman Art Library, London/New York: Bibliothèque Nationale, Paris clb. Corbis: Dean Conger cla (land), Gianni Dagli Orti cb, Ted Spiegel br (dome); Getty Images: AFP br. iStockphoto.com: traveler1116 crb. Zev Radovan, Jerusalem: bc.

All other images © Dorling Kindersley

For further information see:
www.dkimages.com